Pick Your Battle:
Your Guide to Urban Foraging, Hollywood Movies, Late Capitalism and the Communist Alternative
(a Memoir)

Douglas Lain

First Edition May 2011

ACKNOWLEDGMENTS

I would like to thank Miriam for letting me write about our family, our friends Annie and Rachel for promising not to pursue legal remedy, and my children for being either too young to or uninterested in reading this book.

I would also like to offer a special apology to my son Noah who does not appear in the pages that follow. For the sake of narrative clarity I have combined my two sons Noah and Simon into one character named Simon. Noah is my youngest son, he is six years old, and he always makes sure to sit next to me at the dinner table. My choice to eliminate him from this book has nothing to do with my affection for him. I love you, Noah. Sorry, boy.

I also want to thank the 165 people who contributed to the Kickstarter campaign to fund the writing and printing of this book. Charlotte Kelly is an old high school friend who I met through Miriam and she made a very large donation to the project, as did Ken Beare. Ken was the one who originally suggested that I seek funding through Kickstarter, and he is a friend and associate of mine in Portland. On the other hand, I have never met Eileen Workman in person, but I have spoken to her by phone. Ms. Workman made the largest donation to the Kickstarter campaign. She is a former financial banker who is now a committed anti-capitalist. You can find out more about Eileen and her projects at the website sacredeconomics.org, and you can hear my conversation with Eileen at dietsoap.podomatic.com. We spoke in episode number sixty-six.

A special thank you also to the artist Daniel Shea who created the cover image, and to the authors M. K. Hobson and Glen Kirsch who contributed design and editing skills to the book. M. K. Hobson designed the cover and interior of the book while Glen Kirsch copyedited the manuscript.

3

Introduction to Pick Your Battle

When I sought funding for the writing and printing of this book through Kickstarter, I described the book as an exploration of urban foraging and Situationist theory, as a radical or even surrealist self-help book, that would offer instructions on urban foraging and dérives while telling the story of my own attempt to revolutionize everyday life. My assumption was that there were people out there who would understand just what Situationist theory was historically and who would be interested in reading a book that attempted to apply the ideas of Guy Debord to today's world of perpetual crisis. My assumption was proved out as there were well over a hundred people willing to help me fund the project.

I want to start this book by offering my thanks to the fine people who contributed to this project.

I also want to begin by describing how, through wandering, foraging, reading, and writing I've come to be as interested in the abstract idea of a juxtaposition as I am in the juxtaposition of Guy Debord's political theory and urban foraging, or as I am in the contradiction between urban life and the life of a forager. I've come to believe that contradiction is the universal principle at work in the modern world, and this book, written as a kind of collage, is a series of repetitions and contradictions around that idea.

Collaging and foraging are similar practices. Both revolve around found objects, both privilege what is ephemeral and excessive, and both emerged historically as traditional methods of production appeared to fail.

In Brandon Taylor's coffee table book *Collage: The Making of Modern Art* the technique of the collage is described as follows:

> "Modernity's fragments, some collages suggest, are its history, its residue; they are what is left over when the great feast of consumption has ended for the day, when trading and exchange have ceased and the people have gone home for a rest. Collage in the fine arts allows us to see that it is somewhere in the gulf between the bright optimism of the official world and its degraded material residue, that many of the exemplary, central experiences of modernity exists."[1]

Consider this:

One of the key backers and participants in this Pick Your Battle project was my neighbor Annie. Annie is a bohemian mother whose three children are friends of my own children, she is a friend to my wife, and a friend of mine. Beyond all of this Annie is an experienced urban forager and naturalist with a degree in "Cross-cultural Perspectives on Community, Wellness and Sustainability." When she heard that I was embarking on a foraging project, when she watched my YouTube video that called for anarchy and abundant cities, Annie volunteered her time and expertise to help me with my effort.

We wandered the Woodstock neighborhood together; her family met up with my own at Woodstock Park and the ten of us set off up Reedway together. We crossed 52nd St, and when Reedway jogged to the left at 52nd, we continued straight ahead into the weedy and unpaved alley that divided the block between Reedway and Ramona. There were quite a few alleys like the Reedway Alley, and once we crossed 52nd, our foraging prospects improved

---

1) *Taylor, Brandon. "Collage: the Making of Modern Art." Thames and Hudson, New York, 2004*

significantly precisely because there were more unpaved alleys, more fissures in the Woodstock plan. Before Annie joined us, my sons and I had explored these blocks already, and while we hadn't found much to bring home other than dandelion greens, I was sure this was because I was a novice. I could barely distinguish a blackberry bush from a patch of mint, let alone make out which weeds and roots were edible. I took *Edible Wild Plants: A North American Field Guide to Over 200 Natural Foods* with me, but found that the color photographs of cherry blossoms and chickory didn't give a novice like myself much in the way of confidence. Annie had a much easier time of it. "That's Oregon Grape. I sometimes make tea out of it. It's an antioxidant."

"See any plants we could put in a salad? Anything to eat?"

"There are dandelion greens."

Annie's approach to foraging was very much like Brandon Taylor's description of a collage. She would gather St. John's Wort or lemon balm in order to create homemade tinctures and salves. These plants Annie gathered were not meant to replace the food she gained from the agricultural market, but were gathered as medicinal supplements to her industrial diet. However, apart from the extra vitamins or detoxifying effects the plants contained, what Annie received from these medicines was a way to reconnect to the real world. If the commodities in cereal boxes and plastic bags had lost the essential qualities that constituted real food, foraged berries and leaves could fill the gap. What we could easily collect from the alleys in the Woodstock neighborhood acted on us in very much the same way as a homeopathic sugar pills. The power of homeopathic medicines stems from what the pills do not contain. A pill for insomnia will consist of sugar pills that are labeled as caffeine-free, and a pill for an upset stomach will assure you that it does not contain some ingredient that would, if present, cause nausea. These are placebos that announce themselves as such, and

6

yet they work. I've taken them, and found relief through their use, but they work precisely as specters.

> "The specter conceals the piece of the Real which has to be forsaken if reality (in the guise of the Symbolic) is to exist. And it is here, in the spectral supplement, that Zizek locates the foundation or kernel of all ideologies. All of which is another way of saying that reality and ideology are mutually implicated in each other. One cannot exist without the other."[2]

The philosopher Walter Benjamin wrote about the aura of art in the age of modern industrial reproduction, and mourned the passing of this artistic specter as one of the consequences of a mechanized and thereby democratic means of reproduction. The found object as the central element in a collage is that specter returned, just as a blackberry or dandelion leaf represents the specter of nature in an unnatural world.

Brandon Taylor chose Picasso's found object, a paper label from the Magasins du Lauvre department store, as the first illustration for his book. Picasso's painted collage is entitled *The Dream*, and Taylor describes the work, with its references and parodies of Cezanne and Manet, as a dream with multiple meanings. Picasso collaged together this dream in 1909, and perhaps its title points to what is most hopeful about collage and about foraging. These are efforts to expose the specters in our own lives, and the ghosts we find growing on blackberry bushes or that we clip out of life magazine are not invisible. We can see them quite clearly and they challenge us, perhaps not to wake up, but to dream differently.

---

2) *Myers, Tony. "Slavoj Zizek." New York, Routledge, 2003*

Section One: Who are You? (the Dream of the 90s)

Bee Sticker: 1989

According to the *American Heritage Dictionary* a synchronicity is a coincidence of events that seems to be meaningfully related. Conceived in Jungian Theory as an explanatory principle on the same order as causality, a synchronicity is something in the field of everyday life that is freighted with an unexpected meaning. A Synchronicity fills in the gap between the story a person tells himself about his everyday life and the contingent or accidental working out of this story in real time. It is a happening that appears as something more than itself.

If normal causality works on the level of billiard balls smacking into each other, the synchronicities works on the linguistic level. Words don't smack into each other, but relate to each other in symbolic chains, and while Jung originally conceived of a Synchronicity as a intrusion of the irrational into the realm of the rational, or as a disruption of the normal everyday world of cause and effect, on the level of a linguistic meaning the Synchronicity reestablishes a person's everyday understanding by expressing the disruption.

Let me give you an example of a Synchronicity:

During the summer of 1989 I discovered a bumble bee sticker on the cement floor of my friend's basement while secretly washing my blue jeans at two in the morning. I was in my friend's parents' house because in those months between high school graduation and before college, my relationship with my own parents had broken down. There were too many restrictions at home, but my friend's parents seemed okay with anything. For example, I'd been out with my newest girlfriend until around one in the morning. I spent a few hours at Denny's, then a few hours in her 1967 Ford Falcon. I'd come back to my friend's parents house to crash, expecting that there would be no trouble as long as I didn't make too much noise, and so I tried to be quiet as I snuck into their basement. I only had one last thing to do before crashing in their guest room, and I tried to be quiet and quick about it.

I watched my Levis tumble behind a glass bubble and worried about how I would explain standing by their washing machine in nothing but a Hard Rock Cafe T-shirt and a bath towel if Professor Myers should investigate the noise coming from his radiator vent. As my Levis tumbled, a linguistic relationship between my inner experience and the outer world was established. I was in a limbo point between childhood and adulthood, and things were happening that seemed well beyond my control.

My new girlfriend, for instance, had surprised me on the front bench seat of her Ford. She was just the most recent girl in the series of girls who'd been interested in what I might manage in a backseat or on sofa cushions while parents were out. But as I watched suds form behind the glass bubble of the washing machine I realized that she'd changed the game on me. She'd managed to shift the way I perceived her. I had desired her before, and now I hardly knew what I wanted.

In Lacan's seminar *The Ethics of Psychoanalysis*, he introduced his idea of *jouissance* as something opposed to mere pleasure, and something quite apart from desire. Desire is defined by what is missing. It is a drive defined by language, by the symbolic order of a person's society. Desire always seeks its object, and the arrival of that object is always made possible by something outside.

"Man's desire is the Other's desire. The subject desires only in
so far as it experiences the Other itself as desiring ..." [3]

Looking back I can easily trace how the desire of the Other
directed me to my new girlfriend in 1989. She was the ex-girlfriend
of my best friend, the very best friend whose house I was living
in during the limbo time of 1989. I'd discovered my desire for her
during the final months of my senior year, when she'd been dating
my friend.

The three of us were in the same drama class at Palmer, the two
of them had been paired together for an acting exercise, and after
I watched them perform a scene from Neil Simon's *Barefoot in the
Park* I knew what I wanted.

CORIE: I've got so much to say to you, darling.

PAUL: (*Taking more clothes out of the suitcase*) So have I, Corie ... I got
all the way downstairs and it hit me. I saw everything clearly for the
first time. (*He moves up left to behind the couch.*) I said to myself, this
is crazy ... crazy ... It's all wrong for me to run like this ... (*he turns to
Corie*) And there's only one right thing to do, Corie.

CORIE: (*Moving to him*) Really, Paul? What?

PAUL: (*Jubilantly*) You get out!

CORIE: (*Holding him*) Paul, you're ice cold ... you're freezing ... what
have you been doing?

PAUL: (*Pulls up his pants leg revealing his stockingless foot*) What do you
think I've been doing? (*He puts his foot up on the seat*) I've been walking
barefoot in the goddamn park!

Neil Simon's play placed both my best friend and the girlfriend
into the precise roles that best fit my perceptions of them. My best
friend was practical. He made decent if not excellent grades; he
was captain of the Track team. A conventional sort destined for

---

3) *Zizek, Slavoj. "How to Read Lacan," W.W. Norton and Company, 2006*

sameness. It was, in fact, what he strived after. The girlfriend, on the other hand, was often literally barefoot in the halls, and while she was not as boisterous as Corie, while her rebellion was quiet, even shy, conventional sameness simply was not something she was capable of producing, much less something she seemed to want.

This was the framework for the fiction that supported my desire, but washing my blue jeans after our date indicated that the framework was failing. What I'd encountered in her front seat was not the realization of my desire, but an encounter with surplus desire known as *jouissance*.

> "Let's get back to the idea of jouissance as sexual enjoyment, and it's connection with suffering. If you ask someone to tell you about their experience of orgasms, usually they will tell you what a wonderful thing orgasm are. But imagine an experiment: if you were to stop someone having their orgasm just five seconds before they had it, what do you think they would experience? Extreme discomfort and pain."[4]

What is a Synchronicity? It is nothing more than a symptom. That is, it is an image or set of images that covers over the impossible disruption that *jouissance* brings. In the moment of blue jean washing my fuzzy synchronicity appeared in the form of a bumble bee sticker that was stuck impossibly to the concrete floor. This bumblebee was stuck half under the Maytag, and was just visible when I leaned over to open the door and transfer my pants to the dryer.

I recognized the bumble bee sticker as a memory from the previous summer.

In 1988 I'd worked as a caddy at the Broadmoor Hotel and the very same bumble bee sticker had been ubiquitous. The sticker was handed out to club members before they teed off, and this was

---

4) *Hill, Philip, "Lacan for Beginners," Writers and Readers Publishing, 1997*

how caddies and waiters distinguished between a club members, who were likely to tip, and lowly paying customers.

My best friend's parents were not members of the Broadmoor Country Club; they did not even golf. There was no logical reason for one of these bumble bee stickers to enter their house. To find one as I did, for one of these special bees to appear in that moment when I was thinking about the way my new girlfriend's hands fit together, the way her breath had been visible in the front seat of her Ford Falcon, created a situation wherein the bumble bee was freighted with unexpected meaning. The bumble bee became the image that absorbed my real desire and covered over the gap in my desire.

I put my pants in the dryer, and then picked up the bumble bee sticker. Then I placed the bumble bee, sticky side down, on the lid of dryer, and it stayed there.

I watched the bee buzz and vibrate as the dryer whirled.

Losing My Head/Capitalist Zen

Twenty years after the bumble bee, on 11/11 of 2009, I sat behind cubicle walls and slowly came to the realization that I had no head.

I'd been taking calls in a call center for a major telecommunications company for the past six hours, had been taking phone calls in a gray carpeted cubicle for over two years, had therefore been very close to the realization of this abyss for quite awhile, but it was not until 4 p.m. on a Wednesday that this reality finally broke through.

It came on me in waves. First I realized that the sounds—the multitude of greetings and assurances, the television sets that were strategically placed at the center of each pod of cubicles with the volume turned not quite but almost all the way down, the hiss of air conditioning from overhead—all of this together formed something singular. A process of audio syncretism was possible. I could hear a voice. I turned off my phone, took myself out of the flow of incoming calls, and listened to the words I thought I could hear coming out of that buzzing moment inside the vast efficiency of the call center.

"I am."

This moment included my own thoughts. There was no separation between my running commentary on events and the events themselves. I witnessed the white girl with dreadlocks in the cubicle next to mine adjusting her headset and then nervously fiddling with the zipper on her lime green sweat jacket as she worked up the nerve to lie to the customer on the other end of the line, and her words seemed familiar. I could not separate what she was saying about high-speed internet service from what was going on inside my own head. I could not absolve myself from her actions. The universe did not bend to my will, but it did respond to my ideas, and this realization of the relationship between my ideas and the world of my experience was my enlightenment.

Satori. Revelation.

I didn't have a head. Instead of a head I had a room full of cubicles, ringtones, keystrokes, sales pitches, and words. This awareness was attached to my neck, but there was no head. No face.

The cult leader Osho Rajneesh once instructed his followers on how to drop their illusions. He said, "Drop everything. Drop asking, drop deep breathing, drop all activity. Let everything be still and quiet, quiet and empty, as if you are dead, as if you have disappeared. Only emptiness remains. Everything is quiet. Everything is peaceful. Everything is silent. It is in this silence that God comes. This emptiness is the gate through which He enters us. Await, just await, as if you are dead. As if you have disappeared."

This is what happened to me. I stepped away from the queue of incoming calls, stopped trying, and disappeared or died. There was nothing, nobody. I could hold out my hands and see them, I could look down at my feet, but I couldn't see my head. I could not look back that far.

Sitting in my cubicle I realized that my head had disappeared, and having that thought, expressing those words to myself I remembered being five years old in Oakridge, Tennessee and getting an Aquaman doll for Christmas. I remembered twisting his blonde head around and around, spinning his head so the doll moved like the girl who spun her head in the movie *The Exorcist*. I remembered that when Aquaman's head came off his arms and

16

legs popped off too. All of his parts had been held together by a rubber band hidden inside his torso, and when the rubber band broke everything about the toy superhero fell to pieces. I looked at my hands, remembered what it had been like to be five years old in 1976 and have a Super Friend break on me, and my head returned.

I hit the button on the phone and took the next call. Then looked up at the laser-printed reproduction of an anarchist poster that I'd hung on the burgundy wall of my cubicle with thumb tacks.

The poster was an altered Taylorist diagram of an efficient office workspace and an efficient worker. This altered version consisted of dotting that traced the best path for a worker's elbow or hand, it showed how a swivel chair might increase a worker's efficiency, but where the original instructions for efficient movement had been a vandal had written the following words:

"Wake up. Brush Teeth. Drive to Work. Check in. Work. Clock out. Drive Home. Sleep. Wake up. Brush Teeth. Drive to Work. Check in. Work. Clock out. Drive Home. Sleep. Wake up. Brush Teeth. Drive to Work. Check in. Work. Clock out. Drive Home. Sleep ..."

There were two ways to make the passing of time, the mindless repetition, less painful. The first was to imagine that the situation was temporary, but this was more difficult to do at the age of thirty-eight than it had been a decade earlier.

The second way was to erase or eliminate my subjectivity. If there was no true self, if I could hum, chant, drug, or meditate myself out of existence, then the pain would simply flow through me. It was easy to accomplish. To eliminate myself merely required that I notice the reality behind my mindless repetition. To be self-aware was always to notice the void at the center of my existence. If I could see myself, be aware of my movements, watch my thoughts, watch my feelings, objectively watch myself, the question would eventually arise. Who was it that was objectively watching? And the answer, of course, would be "nobody."

Another method of erasure was to play video games. Specifically what I did was play a game called Roblox. This was a video game for children and my avatar was a blockhead with a block body and a rifle in a blocky hand. I marched this hollow figure through geometric landscapes looking to kill, to blow apart, the alphabet blocks that made up my enemies' bodies. It was an addiction that always left me feeling sick with adrenaline and fear when I finished, only I never did finish. This game didn't have an ending.

I spent my nights pursuing my fellow blockheads, all of us outwardly identical, all of us hollow inside—just empty shells with smiles and eyes painted onto yellow plastic. No, these eyes were digitized onto virtual surfaces meant to resemble plastic blocks, and yet this game seemed more authentic than my daily commute or the scripted conversations I engaged in for money.

What was I striving after by playing this repetitive game? What did it signify when my square bullets reached their targets? Did I shoot the avatars on the screen or did the logic of the game merely move through me in order to complete a relationship that had been defined in advance?

> "When I think over the weirdest of all things I can think of, do you know what it is? Nothing." [5]

In the early 70s, after a hundred or more attempts at revolution, after political solutions had failed, there was a turning away from thought and from reason. This turning away coincided with the ascendancy of a popularized eastern or mystical approach to life. Zen was given as a way to cope with, or perhaps to personally transcend, capitalism.

---

5) Watts, Alan, "On Nothingness," *Reflected Flicks (distributed on YouTube)*, 2008

One good example of this trend toward the void or the personal is Hugh Prather's collection of hippie aphorisms entitled *I Touch the Earth and the Earth Touches Me*. According to Wikipedia Hugh Prather is "an author, minister, and counselor whose philosophy emphasizes gentleness and forgiveness." He is a proponent of rational emotive behavior therapy, which itself advocates a kind of stoicism. Reading Prather's book nearly forty years after its initial publication, the book appears to be dated precisely to the extent that it seems to be about what it is to be human. There is a hint of neurosis in the text, a touch of R. D. Laing. Still, Prather presents his personal notebook not as a book of answers, but as an "asymptotic shot at life." He tells the reader that if the ideas in his book seem challenging or off then the reader should reject them.

"You are the authority on what is good for you."[6]

But it is important to recognize hidden in this imperative to be one's own authority. This is, in fact, a defensive maneuver. Prather is insisting not that we remain alert and critical, but that we limit our response to his text to a binary reaction. We should either accept or reject what he tells us. There is no way to contest the text. Engaged effort to contest social meanings is precisely what he is writing against.

Prather says, "A problem does not have to be thought about in order to be solved."

Prather says, "I can reverse almost everything I've written and it is equally true."

Prather says, "No one thing is more profound than anything else."

This is not an open approach to knowledge. Prather's book laid down a dogma that would define thought for decades to come. The injunction?

---

6) Prather, Hugh. "I Touch the Earth and the Earth Touches Me". Doubleday, 1972

"Abandon thought. Do not struggle."

If you go far enough in this direction you will either levitate or turn into a smiley face blockhead willing to pick up any weapon in the endless war against subjectively experienced real life.

> "But in a culture so overloaded, where we already suspect if not know that its goal is psychoanalysis in reverse, to make the parts of us that think into ones that don't think, one thing that we can do is just tune out. So many of us do that in one form or another. We take the culture and simply try to tune out as much of it as we can, but there is a flaw in this strategy. The fact is that no other culture before this one was so pervasive. Even the word 'culture' is a problem. There was a time when 'culture' meant going to the things created by us folks as opposed to nature. But where is nature now?" [7]

This need to escape ourselves, this urge to become objects, is acted out everywhere. This is the compulsion behind the New Age phenomena known as "The Secret." The imperative to give up on subjective desires and efforts sets up this solution: Offer up your desires to an impersonal force that will grant you satisfaction as long as your desires are uncomplicated or pure. The solution isn't to get your hands dirty by engaging in the world, but rather to purify your thoughts so that the universe or God will give you what you want.

Of course you will never be able to think purely enough. This is a superego injunction that, just like all the others, is impossible to fulfill. Every thought always contains its opposite, not as a balanced equation that negates itself, but rather as a function of its linguistic character. In order for a word to be meaningful it must refer to at least two other words. One word, the synonym, is conjured as a means of support, and another, the antonym, defines the original word negatively.

---

7) Roderick, Rick. "Philosophy and Human Values," The Teaching Company on VHS, 1990

Our race to destroy our identities is pervasive. This is why lol cats or posters of dogs playing poker are so popular. We long for an escape from the symbolic or social world. To identify with a calico kitten, or to laugh at a Doberman wearing a green visor, expresses a desire for uncomplicated desire. We want an unspoiled self-awareness. We want to be able to act in the world without guilt or reflection.

Hugh Prather explained our condition perfectly in 1972:

"I saw Dina at the party tonight. She smiled at me brightly and said, 'This year I decided to give up suffering.'"

Sex on the Beach 1990

In 1992 the Cultural Theorist Celeste Olalquiaga wrote that the phenomena called psychasthenia was the defining experience of modern urban life:

> "Defined as a disturbance in the relation between self and the surrounding territory, Psychasthenia is a state in which the space defined by the coordinates of the organism's own body is confused with represented space." [8]

A good illustration of the psychasthenic experience is a photograph entitled Empty Dream by the Japanese artist Mariko Mori. The photo depicts a beach as a movie set, a beach where both the clean and clear ocean that fills the horizon and the light blue sky above, are elements in a matte painting at the edge of a pool. In the photograph plastic panels and scaffolding are the visible supports for a perfect summer day, and families of tourists frolic on identical purple inner tubes inside the frame. Mori's fantasy image includes mermaids with blue sequin tails and blue hair. There are three of them in the photograph, one in the foreground, one at mid-distance, and one at the horizon. All that can be seen of the third mermaid is her blue tail peeking out of blue water in an artificial sea.

In 1990 I had my own psychasthenic experience. I was 19 years old and attending a liberal arts college in St. Petersburg, Florida. My high school girlfriend had flown Delta from my hometown in

---

8) Olalquiaga, Celeste. *"Megalopolis: Contemporary Cultural Sensibilities"*
University of Minnesota Press, 1992

Colorado to visit me at Eckerd College near Boca Ciega Bay, a place where the sea and sky were always blue.

What I recall from the first day we spent together, our reunion after a summer populated by bumble bee stickers, is the taste of salt water, the way her lime green bathing suit felt in my hand, and finding a somewhat secluded inlet where the water was shallow enough for me to keep my head above water while we were together, but deep enough for my sense of modesty.

For her the juxtaposition between the previous day's Calculus test inside a high school built by Roosevelt's WPA and sex acts that were surrounded by cement boxes, waterfront palm trees, and a UFO-shaped Chapel building with exposed girders in the place of flying buttresses must have been disconcerting, but for me the moment was exactly normal. The actuality of being a 19-year-old college student in yellow Bermuda shorts, the realization of a girlfriend in a green knit bikini was something static and without traction, up to my neck in the ocean and in my full identification with the moment the act became impossible.

In an attempt to make progress we left the beach and started drinking. We did tequila and 7Up slammers with all the other beautiful college coeds in the Iota complex of dormitories. The fizz tickled my nose. I slammed down the shot glass on top of the stainless steel mini-fridge in order to start the reaction, and then raised my glass. My girl friend did the same. She smiled at me, slammed the shot glass, and then swallow the foam that this action produced.

We each went through this procedure about four or five times. It was easy to drink this way.

Let's return for a moment to the artist Mariko Mori as a mermaid. How are we to understand her appearance on an artificial beach? Is she not attempting to blend into the background? Examining

23

Mori's *Empty Dream* is a bit like reading Martin Hanford's *Where's Waldo*. Finding her image is the point of the photo, but while from a naive realist perspective her appearance as a mermaid breaks with the reality of the rest of the photograph; it is in fact her way of renouncing reality and mimicking the constructed environment.

After all, the landscape in Mori's photograph is a real artificial beach. The Seagaia Ocean Dome opened in 1993 and provided a blue sky for tourists until 2007. The landscape in the photograph was real; it was a real fake. The mermaids in her photograph, these bodies that only exist as images, blend right in.

And the story of sex on the beach, the tale of swallowing foamy tequila slammers in a desperate attempt to escape from my body and get fucked, ends badly. My girlfriend couldn't stomach the scene and her mad laughter slowly turned to inconsolable crying.

We ended up moving from the dim rotating light in the television lounge of the Iota Complex to the harsh glare of a toilet stall. I recall holding her long blonde hair so that she could vomit cleanly, but all that came out of her was a retching noise and more salty tears.

The difference between psychasthenia and psychogeography is the difference between identifying with your image and establishing a critical distance from it. This critical distance doesn't allow you to find a way to the real thing on the other side of the image, but just helps you to get your hands on the image as image.

The difference between the failure of that first night with my girlfriend and the success of our mutual courtship the previous summer was that the failure in Florida was easy. The failure happened naturally and seemed fully real, but the success of our mutual seduction in the summer of 1989 began as a fiction.

We documented the process of our mutual seduction as a music video made with my father's Sony Super 8 video camera. The montage shows the two of us being beautiful and young and dancing together in the park, and walking over interstate pedestrian bridges. She pretends to play a violin during the video and I just manage to look like I'm playing a guitar by a back yard fence on Nevada Ave. We spent a few days videotaping each other while wandering through downtown Colorado Springs. Then we spent few days editing the images together. And if I had to pick a particular moment when we fell for each other it would be the three and one-half minutes of videotaped images that we put together in order to illustrate the song *Season's Cycle*. And perhaps if my marriage were ever to get into trouble, what we'd need is not a therapist or some method to get in touch with our true feelings, but a functioning VHS player.

Another argument against spontaneity and originality is the fact that our first kiss was also a repetition.

It happened when were wandering my neighborhood past curfew. She was seventeen and I was eighteen, it was one o'clock in the morning, and we were standing on a play structure on the playground of my old elementary school, on a bridge made from four stainless steel chains and planks of dark maple wood. After a summer of flirtation I finally put my arms around her, leaned in for a kiss, and missed. The planks of wood shifted, I stumbled, and nearly fell. We had to walk across the bridge, find a steadier place to stand, before the kiss could be consummated, and by then it was no longer a impetuous move, but an intentional act. She'd accepted my earlier attempt, but I'd missed, and so a fully mutual second kiss was also, in this way, our first.

Turning the Camera Around

Here's the premise: Subjectivity arises out of the recognition of what is missing from the field of vision.

For example, in Hollywood movies this identification is achieved through the employment of the shot/reverse shot sequence and a violation of the one hundred and eighty degree rule.

Wikipedia defines this rule as "a basic guideline for filmmaking that states that two characters (or other elements) in the same scene should always have the same left/right relationship to each other. If the camera passes over the imaginary axis connecting the two subjects, it is called crossing the line. The new shot, from the opposite side, is known as a reverse angle."

An example of the shot/reverse shot sequence can be found in the film *Willy Wonka and the Chocolate Factory*. Wonka leads the children down a hallway to a small door that, once opened, magically transforms into a giant iron door. The perspective reverses, breaks the rule, as the children step forward into the chocolate room and we linger on their astonishment. Another shot/reverse shot sequence is employed. First we scan the entire field of candy treats, take in the chocolate river, and then the shot reverses onto Charlie's open mouthed expression of hunger and joy.

"The viewer experiences shot one as an imaginary plenitude, unbounded by any gaze, and unmarked by difference. It is thus a site of enjoyment. However, almost immediately, the viewing subject becomes aware of the limitations of what it sees—aware, that is, of an absent field. At this point shot 1 becomes a signifier of that absent field, and jouissance gives way to unpleasure. In the moment of unpleasure the viewing subject perceives that it is lacking something." [9]

The establishing shot is of the chocolate factory with its unregulated pleasures: Mushrooms with whipped cream spots, melons filled with jelly, gummy bears that grow on trees. The next shot, 180 degrees to the left or right, establishes the subject of the gaze; #2 gives us a location for the gaze. Charlie is the subject, and he is located precisely there on the screen and in the narrative that is unfolding.

This is both a suture and it is a cut. Precisely by limiting the image of the real a verisimilitude of subjective experience is achieved. And by pointing the camera away from the object of perception and objectifying the perceiver the subject is created.

I can only understand or grasp this idea of the suture or gap from my own perspective inside this small story that I'm telling. In order to illustrate this gap, I'm going to have to break the rules. I'm going to turn my pen around and tell you something now that should come later. I'm compelled to break the fourth wall and shatter the illusion of a linear narrative even at this point in the text where this narrative hasn't even firmly established itself. I haven't finished explaining how I came to be a wanderer, but despite all the misunderstandings that will inevitably result if I skip ahead, in fact precisely in order to create these misunderstandings, I'm going to tell you about looking for blackberries in an alley off Reedway.

I've reached a point where I have to turn the camera around.

Early on in my foraging adventures a supporter whose business involved the creation of realistic maps through the use of satellite

9) Sarup, Madan, "Jacques Lacan", University of Toronto Press, 1992

photography sent me such a map. He sent me a photograph of the Woodstock neighborhood taken from outerspace with the the hope that by looking down on my neighborhood I could get a better sense of where I lived. His map did help. I discovered, among other things, that my neighborhood was a checkerboard where the white and blue rectangular roofs of residential ranch houses competed with the more curved shapes of planted deciduous trees. My neighborhood was made up of light green square lawns, darker green circles of tree tops, and a million white box tops separated by black lines of asphalt.

Alleys showed up on this satellite photo as narrow brown lines that usually continued on where the black lines stopped. I lived on a series of boxes connected by as well as separated by roads and lawns.

In the third world of lived experience, as opposed, say, to the hyper-real two dimensional world of the television or internet images, neutral space appears as nature. It is easy to see how the space in a cafe or public library is constructed or produced, but the ways in which a forest or swamp is produced is more difficult to spot. A crack in a sidewalk where a dandelion or strip of grass has pushed through, a pocket of protected swamp land, an alley full of blackberry bushes, all of these are produced spaces, but just how are they produced and to what effect?

In early July a group of us explored these alleys. There were seven of us searching. My three boys, my wife Miriam, her friend Annie, and Annie's son, Kenneth. And what we found were blackberry bushes.

They were everywhere. And one short alley was completely overrun with them. We had to duck down to get past the vines and branches of bushes that had not yet produced berries or even flowers, but that were so numerous and large that I imagined a superabundant yield would be coming soon. The sunlight was made green by leaves and vines, and the air under the canopy was moist.

I recall that we stopped in this alley, under the blackberry leaves, between the prickly branches, for several minutes, and we discussed the Pick Your Battle project and how very trendy urban foraging was becoming. Anne informed me that *Willamette Week* had recently run a feature on it. The practice was no longer associated with dumpster diving and ecoterrorism, but with knitting and backyard chickens.

I imagined the *Willamette Week* photo shoot. Imagined a clutch of young women in blue and brown coats, women with dreadlocks, underneath our blackberry bush canopy. I saw them reaching up with hands clad in fingerless wool gloves. I imagined them picking ripe fruit, imagined blackberry juice dribbling down their confident chins. They were laughing with each other, wiping purple juice off each other's faces, and then running through the alley in a race for more.

"The problem is that some of these bushes are so overgrown that the berries won't get any sun. It will be slow to produce ripe fruit," Annie told me.

"Even if half or a third of the berries are good, these bushes will produce more than we'll know what to do with."

My imagination didn't settle down into a coherent image, but was a fragmented orgy of berries, fashion, and the beautiful geek girls I'd seen in American Apparel advertisements. I imagined these hipster women and immediately envied them for getting to the alley first. Foraging was already popular.

My envy demonstrated how quickly an act that aimed at realizing a desire could be turned or could slip into an act of seeking to be desired.

Writing about Disneyland Neville Wakefield commented:

> "It is the imagination of the child that is conceived as the past and future utopia of adults. The child is seen to represent a state of nature forfeited by the complexity of adult life. The omnipresence of animals within the Disney world also helps to reinforce the suggestion that it is nature itself that pervades and determines the whole complex of social relationships." [10]

Perhaps the alleys truly are neutral. Certainly these fissures are nothing like the flat images constructed inside Disney, but the neighborhoods we live in are, more and more, like theme parks. I live in 1960s suburbia—a neighborhood lined with ranch houses built in that era, houses that emphasize the garage and the lawn while deemphasizing ornamentation. Perhaps these sorts of neighborhoods could be said to represent the last gasp of modernism. Thirty blocks away my friends live in a mid 20th century neighborhood where a sense of urban community is inscribed into Craftsman Style bungalows that line their block. In Beaverton and Lake Oswego there are homes that were built in the 80s and 90s and these represent nothing so much as the victory of late 20th century globalism. These homes aren't inscribed with a utilitarian aesthetic, but are simply receptacles for whatever current lifestyle can be squeezed into the back of trucks and delivered. Disposable and transitory, these Plexiglass wonders are the ahistoric conclusion of the history of the 20th century.

Disneyland is everywhere, and the rule is that there are no seams. There is one flat image of an American Utopia that appears in a thousand or a million guises. The rule is that we must never turn the camera around on this image. We must never expose the gap.

---

10) *Wakefield, "Postmodernism: The Twilight of the Real," Pluto Press, 1990.*

Fact or Fiction

My wife Miriam was the teenage girl who brought me bumble bee stickers, who played the part of Corie in a Palmer High School drama class production of *Barefoot in the Park*, and who got sick from tequila shooters. She is now the 39 year old woman who, after reading my accounts of those school days together, was quick to point out all the details that diverged from her own memories of our time together.

For example, she claims that the incident with tequila shooters took place during her second visit to Eckerd College and not on the first night of her first visit. Also, she doesn't recall being in my drama class at all, but did play opposite my best friend in a high school stage production.

In an effort to set things straight, let me start the story of our wedding with a detail that I will confess at the outset is wrong. Still, the image of Christmas lights shaped like cows, semi-transparent plastic Bessies wearing Santa Claus hats and lined up along an electric wire, has been seared into my memory. While I realize that Miriam actually purchased these Christmas lights during our honeymoon in Newport, I must start with this image, perhaps precisely because this image is wrong. The cow-shaped Christmas tree lights serve as a good reminder as to the fictional character of memory, so let me start there.

Standing on the fourth floor balcony outside my studio apartment, counting the plastic cows on a string of novelty Christmas tree lights that were twined around the iron balcony rail, I felt that I was not ready to be married. It was not that I wasn't ready to be committed to my girlfriend but that I was discombobulated by the passage of time, the forward momentum, that a wedding suggested. My best friend from high school and I stood under the eave of my apartment and inhaled smoke from Swisher Sweet cigars. We discussed the then recent suicide of Guy Debord and why my life seemed to be speeding up.

"What does it mean that he came down on the side of suicide?" I asked.

"You're 23 years old, Doug. You've been with Miriam for five years. This is hardly sudden," my friend said. I objected that he wasn't listening to me, and he rejoined with the observation that he was listening perhaps too well.

Of course, he hadn't read Guy Debord's work, but I'd mentioned it enough that he knew of it. My friend speculated that Debord's suicide was an indication that thought and reason had limits, and that the great Marxist thinker had been consumed by personal demons. That is, Debord's suicide was largely meaningless. It was just another personal tragedy.

I stubbed out my Swisher Sweet on the brick wall and watched sparks drift down onto the Astroturf carpet that covered the concrete floor of the balcony. I stepped on the sparks and searched for the right words so as to object.

"You're always pushing everyday life outside of history," I said. "You buy into this idea that reality is small and local."

My friend coughed politely into his hand. He looked at his cigar and then licked his lips. "It's a little dry," he said. Then he said, "I don't know what that means. Reality is local? Is that some sort of

New Age slogan? I don't know what you're saying and I doubt you do either."

What I meant when I accused my high school friend of pushing everyday life out of history was that he was reducing Guy Debord to the level of a warm human being who had probably committed suicide because he was personally depressed. That put Debord outside of the succession of images that constituted history. In order for Debord to be depoliticized he first had to be made real.

Everyone Says I Love You

The question of where and how we would get married was solved for us by the dogma of Miriam's then chosen church. When Miriam wasn't living with her mother on a Sufi Commune, she was raised in her father's Orthodox Christian church. Orthodox Christianity traces its faith and doctrine right back to Saul on the Road to Damascus, and even a cynic like myself had to admit that this church with its Icons and candles and song, was much closer to some sort of visceral or living God than any other Christian church I'd encountered.

I recall visiting Miriam's church and watching the curtain behind the Orthodox priest who was singing to God while his congregation stood in rows and sang back to him. The air was foggy with incense and I got the impression that we were calling God to us. At any moment the priest would pull the curtain aside and we'd be overwhelmed by His living presence. I tried to think of what God might look like or what He might be doing behind that curtain while He waited for us to act. While right now it's easy to think of Frank Morgan and Oz, in the moment I wondered if the curtain would be pushed aside and I'd find an icon, a life-sized icon, of Christ looking out to the congregation. Or maybe there would be another curtain behind the first one, and then another, and then another curtain behind that one—different colored curtains layered red, purple, green—all the way back to the far wall.

Miriam and I couldn't get married in the Orthodox church

unless I converted to her faith, but I felt that such a conversion was impossible. I didn't believe in their God, just their curtain, and unless the priest was willing to take me past that barrier, unless they could show me God directly, I couldn't sign up.

So rather than marrying into Miriam's faith we married under the sign of my cynicism. We found a nondenominational church that we could rent by the hour, purchased 100 pairs of Groucho glasses, and found a cellist who knew how to play the song *Everyone Says I Love You* from the Marx Brothers movie *Horsefeathers*.

And we wrote our own vows:

"I feel as though I'm a domino in the chain of history. That is, I don't believe in marriage as an institution, but despite this, I am getting married. Something—an historical force, the will of my parents and grandparents—is acting both through me and against me, and I would resist this moment, I'd take a stand against it, except for you, Miriam."

"I don't believe in marriage but I believe in you, and the way I feel about you. The way I feel when I am with you."

Slavoj Zizek summed up the function of my disavowal in his book *The Plague of Fantasies*:

> "The lesson is therefore clear: an ideological identification exerts a true hold on us precisely when we maintain an awareness that we are not fully identical to it, that there is a rich human person beneath it: 'not all is ideology, beneath the ideological mask, I am also a human person' is the very form of ideology, of its practical efficiency'."[11]

The song played at our wedding as we walked down the aisle together, was *Everyone Says I Love You*. In the movie *Horsefeathers* this is the song that each Marx Brother sings or performs for the

---

11) *Zizek, Slavoj, "Plague of Fantasies". Verso Press, 1997*

blonde bombshell Thelma Todd. First the bland Zeppo sings it to her straight. Thelma Todd plays the role of the college widow who allows Zeppo to bring her breakfast in bed. Zeppo sings to her and feeds her with a spoon, and yet despite the intimacy of this act the possibility that the bed was shared is a negative possibility.

Chico sings to her while giving her an ersatz piano lesson, and Chico's song is absurd and silly, but it is when Groucho sings "… I Love You" that the song is reduced to an ode to animalistic lust. It becomes a song about the reproductive instinct, and only after this debasement can Harpo, who earlier whistled the song to his horse in a display of naive Zoophilia, play the song without words. When Harpo plays it out on his harp he is able to express animalistic reproductive lust as human romance, and it is through Harpo that we return to the original intention of the song. Harpo's version of simple love works where Zeppo's did not, and in this same way belief without belief can be seen to function as well.

How to Write Instructions on Wandering

According to the Canadian website writersblock.ca "the old prohibition on directly addressing the reader has turned 180 degrees."

The turn around was brought on by the need in technical writing to convey procedural information in a conversational style. While historically an author avoided the second person as it signaled bad breeding and a lack of sophistication, today's technical society demands the writer directly address the reader. The need to relay instructions as directly as possible has superseded stylistic concerns about the use of the second person.

In literary works, especially stories written during what you think of as the late capitalist era, the second person became increasingly popular. Authors who wanted to deploy unreliable narrators or who wanted to incorporate their own real biographies into fictional works often turned to the second person in order to force the reader to identify with a protagonist despite his deviance, despite his unsympathetic behavior, and despite his unreliability.

You will employ the second person for both practical and literary reasons. You need to tell the reader what to do. You need to command the reader to implement the ideas in your book, and you hope that by employing the second person you can win the reader's sympathy without going to the trouble of writing a sympathetic account. Before you begin you'll build confidence in the reader by quoting a respected expert:

> "Human beings are not fully conscious of their real lives. Groping
> the dark, overwhelmed by the consequences of their acts, at
> every moment groups find themselves faced with outcomes
> they had not intended." [12]

You are skeptical, even suspicious, of the idea that one can
directly implement old techniques of liberation. Instead you want to
revise and reconstruct these techniques. Not in order to make the
results more palatable for today's audiences, but so that these old
approaches might constitute some sort of threat. A virus mutates
not to keep up with fashion, but in order to bypass the system's
immune system and cause an infection. Your task is to bypass the
rules of everyday life and cause an infection there. Old weapons left
behind on the battlefield might be put to use, but keep in mind that
there is no living revolutionary tradition.

In order to alter the technique known as the *dérive*, which is,
after all, only "the dropping of your usual motives for movement
and action and letting yourself be drawn by the attractions of the
terrain and encounters you find as you wander" you'll have to take
the following steps.

1. Consider the origin of *dérive*: This kind of wandering can be
   traced back to the surrealists and their fascination with chance
   encounters. As these artists sought an escape route out of the
   ideological matrix of what was merely real they turned against
   reason and toward dreaming. Free associations, chance
   encounters, synchronicities, random juxtapositions, these
   were all put into service for a surrealist revolution that never
   materialized as anything more substantial than art.

2. The Situationists International developed their version of

---

12) Debord, Guy, "On the Passage of a Few Persons Through a Rather Brief Unity
of Time," Ken Kabb Trans., Bureau of Public Secrets, www.bopsecrets.org, 2003

wandering not as a way to set up chance encounters, but as a "mode of experimental behavior linked to the conditions of urban society." That is, the SI conceived of wandering as both a dream and as a critique.

3. The *dérive*, like history, must unfold through a dialectical process conceived as resolving antagonisms by embracing paradoxes. There is no way to balance out the antagonism between a master and a slave, but this opposition can be synthesized into an oxymoronic enslavement of masters. Christianity, for instance, created just such a resolution to this basic antagonism. Christ is the human God whose heroism is only achieved through his suffering, mortification, and self-sacrifice.

   The antagonism between materialism and spirituality was resolved by the bourgeoisie oxymoronically as capitalism's commodities disguise their sublime or divine characteristics in order to achieve domination by appearing as dumb ordinary material objects.

4. Dream a dream that interprets itself.

5. Critique the urban environment as you are dominated by it.

6. Remember that the Situationists themselves felt that they were dead to the world, or if not quite dead then they felt they were separated from life. It was from this position of separation that they set off to find adventure. They didn't develop their techniques in order to set themselves up as stars, but rather hoped that they might break from the need for stars as they wandered.

7. Drop your everyday relations, your everyday motives, and set out on foot. Start again. Pretend that you're 18 again. Leave home. Start over.

8. Don't forget to write.

Drifting

I set out to wander the Woodstock neighborhood without conscious purpose, headed out into the built environment in order to see where it led me, and in order to be sure to be aimless I started my journey by going wherever the arrows pointed. I was in the parking lot of a strip mall, between Safeway and Bi-Mart, and beneath my feet the white arrow pointed north. I walked toward the exit, and then turned to follow a forest green Volkswagen station wagon that was driving into the parking lot. When I reached the double doors of the supermarket I stopped.

I was the red dot on a map. I was exactly there, a fixed point. I didn't know where to go next.

The concept of confronting the built environment directly, of intervening in everyday life, has a multi-faceted history. The *dérive* or "drift" may have originated in the middle of the twentieth century in Paris, but many others have played with the concept since then. In 1970, a woman artist named Adrian Piper took to the street after she saw how traditional art galleries and museums were faltering. She concluded that if the art world as she'd known it was crumbling this was because the capitalist structure on which these institutions relied was also giving way. Her response was to quit producing conceptual art installations and instead perpetrate what she called catalytic actions. She adorned a polo shirt laden with white paint, hung a "wet paint" sign around her neck, and set off to shop at Macy's.

According to Wikipedia, Adrian Piper is a philosopher as well as an artist. Her confrontational stunts at Macy's apparently, in some small way, informing her development of a "Kantian conception of the self [that] accords priority to freedom, autonomy and moral obligation over the satisfaction of desire and the maximization of utility." But while Macy's may have been able to deliver Ms. Piper to a firm conception of her self, the Safeway parking lot was for me a difficulty.

I zigged and zagged between parked cars, and worried that I might spend my entire afternoon bouncing around the parking lot like a pinball. I followed another painted arrow to my left, then trailed behind a college student whose uniform of a purple Izod shirt and khaki shorts somehow attracted me. He was talking on a smart phone and I followed him around the corner of the Safeway, and then stopped when I found him pacing in front of the dumpster. He just wanted a private corner where he could talk to his girlfriend or his boss or his mother.

I walked around him, squeezed between the dumpster and the brick wall of the Safeway, and then stopped one more time when I reached a high voltage junction box. I stood there and waited.

Psychogeography is meant to offer a violent emotive possession over the streets. Exotic and exciting treasures were to be found in the city by drifters able to conquer her. But standing by the junction box, watching the traffic slowly pass by, I could only muster a critical gaze.

> "I'm tempted to, uh, knock on the door of this house with a wooden welcome sign. To take it literally. But that welcome sign actually means the exact opposite of what it says. The welcome sign means 'Stay Away.'" —*Recorded note to myself during my drifting.*

In 1991, I worked for an environmental organization called OSPIRG. I was 20 years old and they sent me out into these built environments in Portland as a part of a search for environmental types. My job was to wander residential streets, examine the ranch houses and bungalows, and find good liberals willing to hand over checks.

Wandering those same streets nearly twenty years later it is as if nothing has changed. By continuing to wander the urban forest of Portland, remaining with the Alders and Oaks, I am always caught in my memory. Or more precisely, I am always stuck in my same alienation. Walking along Ramona in 2010, stopping outside an orange raised ranch style house, staring at the dark red garage door that someone left slightly ajar, I sense a female presence inside. I flash on a memory of a memory. A woman in business attire, maybe a pantsuit, a faceless woman whose ordered life was contained inside a raised ranch like this one. Or maybe I'm remembering a woman in a tweed jacket and a brown pencil skirt who lived in a Frank Lloyd Wright-style Prairie house in Southwest Portland. Or maybe she was wearing polyester pants and a purple plush robe and lived in a converted International House of Pancakes in Beaverton.

In any case, there was a presence. I could feel it as I stood on the sidewalk not daring to look in. I stood on the street and strained to hear her voice inside. I tried to remember what relationship I might have had with her when I met her before. I must have met her when I was working for OSPIRG. Or maybe she was one of my friend's mothers back in high school. Perhaps she was the woman who lived next door to my family when I was just a baby. The woman who told me about reincarnation and served me store-bought chocolate chip cookies on a crystal plate. She told me that I'd had lived before, maybe. She told me that I might have been somebody else before I was me. This was back in 1976, in Colorado, in what was probably a converted farmhouse.

I stood outside this house, this orange raised ranch style house, and felt that some part of my history, some unknown and inaccessible part of my life, was in the garage. There was a woman from my past in the garage, or maybe in the kitchen.

This was my delusion, and it was a long standing one. I could almost remember a time when these American neighborhoods, these series of square yards and square houses with triangle roofs had been integral to real life. Some woman had, perhaps long ago, told me a secret and I'd just forgotten it over the years. And if I could remember what she said I'd be whole again.

Wandering through the Woodstock neighborhood, moving between the lush lawns and gardens of Portland's private houses, it seemed that each home was the same as the next. These atomized spaces were alike if in no other way than in their very individuality. There were a great many trees around me, meant to create a sense of continuity and identity in a place where no real identity could be found. The poplars and sequoias, the urban forest, obscured what was a material alienation. Driving by rather than walking, a person might be taken in by the greenery and imagine they were in the natural world.

I was meant to be grateful for all the trees, for the stalks of corn that peeked over tall privacy fences. I was meant to be glad for the plums and apples I found rotting on the sidewalks and in the gutters.

In 1991, when I worked as a canvasser going door-to-door to save the environment, I would frequently sit with my clipboard in my lap and ponder the street signs and painted lines. I recall a specific moment when I wrote my first note to the world while sitting on a curb outside a purple Arts and Crafts bungalow on Hawthorne. I turned my back to the windsock and chimes, all that good liberal Karma, and started writing.

I turned over a toxic toy factsheet printed on yellow recycled paper and wrote on the back with a Bic Round Stic pen with medium blue ink. I lit a hand rolled cigarette that was a mix of tobacco and marijuana, took a drag, and tried to put down my thoughts about how the world, the houses and streets, the sprinkler system and perfect lawns, was communicating with me.

I surveyed the progressive tranquility around me, the late 20th century update on a Norman Rockwell painting of an America with perfectly unkempt lawns and sunlit fuel efficient station wagons in the drive. I smoked my half joint and thought about it all. I smoked until I was evaporated and all that was left was a flow of information.

A disjointed critique.

Everything was meaningful. The way the pen felt in my hand, my awkward handwriting, the way the cool summer afternoon air felt in my lungs. I drew a coughing spiral of a flower-petaled apocalypse on the back of the toxic toy factsheet.

That first note went something like this:

"Hello, world. I am nobody until I get my Prozac. Nothing except for a brand new mist green Ford Taurus. I am nobody until I get my paycheck or until the girl in the street cafe smiles at me."

I took another hit and then realized I didn't know how I was going to distribute my work. It had to be put out there immediately. Maybe I'd leave it in somebody's mailbox or slip it under somebody's door? Or maybe I'd leave it under the windshield wiper of somebody's orange VW van. In the end, I searched out a convenience store that was on my route and purchased a roll of masking tape. I quickly pulled out a long strip of tape, enjoying the sound of the quick separation, and made a frame for my first message. I stuck my note to the world to a telephone pole.

Later that summer, I attended a film festival in Telluride, Colorado. The town had functioned under the festival's banner since 1974, and in September of 1991 every path, shop, hotel, and grocery was just one component of a what was no longer a community but a theater lobby. We the tourists, the attendees, had but one goal. We were there to watch. Every spectator was to take in as many films as possible. And if one could figure out a way to watch two or more films at the same time (maybe catching the first ten minutes of River Phoenix in *Dog Fight*, then sneaking off to watch *The Rapture* for thirty minutes, and then finally ending up watching Irene Jacob be beautiful and confusing in something called *The Double Life of Veronique*) then one was implicitly encouraged to do so. The only caveat was that you could not admit to having cheated.

I was still writing notes to the world and taping them up in public space. I wrote my 200th note outside a cafe at this festival, after having read the summaries of the three films while waiting for my latte and thereby saving myself the trouble of seeing them. Outside the coffee shop I taped this note to the underside of an abstract sculpture constructed from a bicycle wheel and a trumpet. The sculpture resembled either a satellite dish or a UFO but was neither of these objects.

From my 100th note I wrote:

> "Evidence for the Festival's complicity in the takeover of humanity by aliens is everywhere. Every film, every artwork, every paper toilet seat cover left behind in every hotel or theater bathroom is a coded message from our new masters. We only need eyes to see the obvious when it is right in front of us."

Nineteen years later, I did not have any masking tape or factsheets, but stood outside an orange and red raised ranch style house and considered how time seemed to stand still.

> "The Bourgeoisie unveiled irreversible time and imposed it on society only to deprive society of its use. Once there was history, but there is no longer any history because the class of owners of the economy, who cannot break with economic history, must repress any other use of irreversible time as representing an immediate threat to itself." [13]

---

13) *Debord, Guy. "Society of the Spectacle," Donald Nicholson-Smith Trans., New York, Zone Books, 1995*

In 2010, I put my mp3 recorder up to my face, held it up to my ear as if it was a cellphone. This subterfuge allowed me to speak aloud without feeling awkward or odd. I could record my reactions to the built environment around me, but no words came.

I spotted a sign, a real sign, as I turned the corner onto Southeast 28th. The sign read "Refresh: Coca-Cola," and I felt relieved. Up to that point I'd only found private spaces. There had been no place to stop, or to stretch out. There had been nowhere to rest, but under the sign of Coca-Cola I could find a moment of respite.

I went into what turned out to be a cocktail lounge and asked for the cola, and the bartender told me that I didn't have to pay. Coca-Cola without booze was so inexpensive it didn't make sense to ask for money at all. The time it would save if I didn't pay was worth more than the money.

The bar was minimalist. The windows inside were high, well above eye level, and I could not see street but only where the light came in. The walls were curved concrete, and the track lighting and tall aluminum chairs communicated a graceful and utilitarian aesthetic. It was a place where one was meant to be seen, and not an appropriate pit stop for a sweating middle-aged slacker toting a knapsack.

I sat at a table outside the bar regardless and flipped through Debord's *The Society of the Spectacle*. I tried to ferret out just what a situation was. Was a situation something real, or just something willed? Was it enough to be free of manipulation, to take hold of your own strings?

Of all the films at Telluride, I recall the movie *The Double Life of Veronique* the most clearly. Veronique was not one person, but two. Her lives were variations on the same theme, and the viewer, the spectator, was led to wonder as he watched each event and its mirror image whether Veronique or her Polish doppelganger

Weronika was really living at all. Was she just a flow of related events? To what extent is anyone free to act out his or her life, and to what extent is that life determined or over-determined?

In 1991, I attended the Telluride film festival with my parents, and the three of us decided to view this picture about Veronica as a family. Afterwards, we stopped off at a cafe and I ordered another latte. My mother chastised me for drinking a caffeinated coffee in the evening while my father suggested that I might have asked for skim milk. I moved away from them, chose to sit at the counter next to a pretty girl who, in my memory, very much resembled the actress from the movie. She had dark wavy hair and wore fine clothing. She seemed to have good prospects. She had the aura of having recently been accepted into a ivy league college about her. In my memory she was as graceful, just as consciously inscribed with gracefulness, as the Coca-Cola cocktail lounge would be nearly twenty years later. I sat down next to her, feeling a bit overwhelmed and a bit greasy as I sat there with her, and was surprised when she struck up a conversation with me.

"Did you see the Kieslowski picture?" she asked.

I confirmed that I had, and then offered that I was interested in the synchronicities in the movie.

According to Wikipedia, the psychoanalyst Jacques Lacan's *objet petit a* (object little-a) stands for the unattainable object of desire. It is sometimes called the object cause of desire. Lacan always insisted for it to remain untranslated "thus acquiring the status of an algebraic sign."

The girl at the Telluride film festival cafe was my *object petit a*. If I could gain her attention then I would be closer to the real me as I saw myself and further away from the me as I felt myself to be. But as she told me that she felt personally connected to Kieslowski's film, when she explained that perhaps she herself had another self, another version of her that she could sense or that was perhaps always sensing her, I started to panic.

"I think I should probably go," I told her.

Twenty years later while rereading *The Society of the Spectacle* I stumbled upon the notion of a constructed situation. They wanted to make moments and not find them. The Situationists were not trying to escape from language, but to speak. They didn't seek uninterpreted reality, but wanted to seize and transform the built environment, to make it real. They would make situations exactly through their own subjective experience of the built environment, and their opposition to it.

When my parents and I reached the sidewalk outside the cafe my father took me by my arm in order to get my attention. He asked me why I had turned away from the girl in the cafe. Did I not understand that she apparently liked me? That she was attempting to have a conversation with me?

I told him that the people in the back, the dishwashers and waiters, were clearly closing up shop. That they were clattering back there in such a way as to communicate. I told him that I'd cut the conversation short due to circumstances beyond my control.

He thought for a moment and then the lights inside the cafe went dark, confirming what had really only been an suspicion on my part. More to the point, it didn't really matter whether or not the cafe was closing down. There could be a hundred more reasons or none at all, but I would never really know what was behind my retreat that night. Was my life, my reactions, determined or my own?

> "The spectacle presents itself simultaneously as society itself, as a part of society, and as a means of unification. As a part of society, it is the focal point of all vision and all consciousness. But due to the very fact that this sector is separate, it is in reality the domain of delusion and false consciousness: the unification

it achieves is nothing but an official language of universal separation."[14]

Drinking my Coca-Cola and reconsidering my journey I realized that, while I'd been drifting, I had not moved the cobblestones aside. I had yet to find the beach.

---

14) Debord, Guy, " Society of the Spectacle", Ken Knabb Trans., Bureau of Public Secrets, 2002

Section 2: Family Life (the Zero Years)

September 11th

While the walks and wandering I've undertaken as a part of this project of picking a battle have been conscious attempts to reorient myself, the walk I remember taking after the attacks on Manhattan was not voluntary. Still, two weeks after September 11th I went on a *dérive* with Miriam, our five year old son Ben, and our three year old daughter Emma. I walked in order to get away from myself. I walked just to keep moving.

Right before the WTC towers fell down I'd finished an essay for an online journal called *Pif Magazine*, an essay that concluded with a quote from Jerome Klinkowitz's preface for the 1972 short story anthology Innovative Fiction. I quoted Klinkowitz quoting Tom Wolfe from his book *The Electric Kool Aid Acid Test*. It was a quote inside a quote then, and now that I repeat it, quoting myself, it is a quote inside a quote inside a quote:

> ""Man has become so rational, so utilitarian, that his perceptions of the world are pale and thin. This is effective for survival, but we've screened out the most wondrous part of experience without knowing it. We're shut off from our own world."" [15]

My essay argued in line with Klinkowitz that the New Fiction of the early 70s, the works of Sukenick, Vonnegut, Barth, Coover and others were attempts to create self-reflection techniques to traverse the blockage, but I also argued that, for the most part, those

---

15) Klinkowit, Jerome, "Innovative Fiction", New York, Dell Publishing Co., Inc, 1972

metafictional writer's did not succeed. I finished it right before the whole country dove into the kind of identity crisis that these 70s writers celebrated as liberating. The essay was published when the whole world appeared as pale and thin, but also in tremendous jeopardy. This walk then was an attempt to get away from all of it, to get away from myself, and as such it was just another symptom of the cultural moment.

I was desperate to reassure my kids, to let them know that the center would hold, and so rather than talk to my wife about practical questions, rather than tell her just exactly when my friend's sister was due to arrive or help her plan for dinner, I focused on pointing out landmarks and cultural markers along the way. It seemed vital that they be able to identify Elvis Presley, whose countenance decorated a storefront window. I wanted them to know what the statue of Abraham Lincoln on Park Street was all about. If our culture was falling apart then it was incumbent on me to reorganize its pieces into something that might cohere after all, at least for a little while. I owed my them this much at least, but the culture I wanted to prop up was working against me.

That August my sister-in-law visited Disneyland and she'd sent my son and daughter Mickey Mouse ears as souvenirs. So that day, a week after the attack, while I was worrying about anthrax and the possibility of nuclear retaliation, while I was trying to set everything back in place, my kids were in their ears.

Ben wanted me to teach him to talk like Mickey, and Emma kept asking me to pretend to be Donald Duck.

We stopped at a park across the street from a Starbucks on 21st, a little park that only took up a quarter of a city block. We stood and stared at the fountain as it burbled away. Water streamed out the mouth of a cement frog, and I realized that I didn't want to talk like Mickey Mouse.

"The Native Americans thought that frogs were good medicine," I told him. "Cleansing medicine."

It was a bluff. I didn't know anything about Indian religions. I'd read a few books, but I didn't really know. I should have stuck with what was familiar. I should have given in to Donald Duck and Mickey Mouse ears.

"Frogs?" my son asked. "How can an animal be medicine?"

"I thought medicine comes from a store," my daughter said.

I didn't know how to explain it to them. How could an animal be medicine? Where do you find medicine if not in a store? I didn't really understand it myself.

We ended up at the train station where we stopped to examine a public artwork: a stainless steel outline of an eye with a steering wheel where the iris should've been. The sculpture is entitled *The Driver's Seat*, and I placed Ben up on the steel chair and looked up at him as he looked out from the center. But, after a moment of letting his gaze define the scene, I changed places with him. I lifted him off the steel throne with its silver sundial for a back and took his place.

All I saw was what I expected to see. I looked out at the brick clock tower on 6th street, at the slogan "Go By Train" written in neon. The land around us was flat. All I saw was dead crab grass, gravel, and asphalt and all the empty space in between these things.

Comcastic

Six years later I started with Comcast. The training room was in the basement of the Beaverton warehouse and we sat under dim fluorescent lights in an air conditioned room without windows. The three tables made a square if you included the projection screen and the trainers: a thirty-something benignly ethnic man who knew how to smile and his younger blonde assistant. These two handed out scented magic markers, and when I was handed a brown marker I took the cap off my pen and took a whiff.

"Do you want to know what the brown markers smell like?" I asked.

"Not particularly," the smiling trainer told me. I glanced at his lovely assistant and wondered if she'd end up getting sawed in half before the three weeks were over.

"What about you?"

"What?" she asked.

"Do you want to know what my brown magic marker smells like?"

"Sure," she said. She didn't even blink. But her boss looked irritated. He was smiling too hard now.

"It smells … like rootbeer."

We were each given a massive three ring binder full of instructions, policies, terminology, and strategies, and then we were given a form to fill out, putting down our name, employee ID #, department ID, and the name of our supervisor as evidence of receipt of this manual. These forms were then collected. The process took about fifteen minutes, and when each of these steps were completed we were informed that the manual was out of date and that we would not be referring to it during the training.

We were asked to introduce ourselves to each other; to state what we wanted to achieve on the job and then tell a story about ourselves. It was a game. The story could be either true or false and the training class would have to guess. Each person would get to vote on whether the story told was a fib or a fact. It was a nod to the form of democracy which revolved around the ferreting out of trivial lies and, in any case, was never to be repeated.

Let's go over it again: Becoming Comcastic started with the signing of a form indicating that you would ignore the old rules, which was followed by a request for a story (preferably a lie) and the full confession of your motives.

"I look at it like this—I'm manipulating them. I'm using them. Besides, it's temporary," my co-worker told me. Mike was a 43 year-old rock and roll scenester and a somewhat recovered junky, who had once opened for the Dandy Warhols. He'd hung around the X-Ray and the Satyricon back in the early 90s, but he was waking up to the fact that he was over forty. He was married with two young boys and he was employed at Comcast.

"I'm using them," he said. "I'm manipulating them."

How did this all work? Perhaps the most sincere player in the game was the always-smiling trainer with his slightly veiled threats and kitten poster self-realization platitudes. At least he had the decency to appear phony. Everyone else was too cool for school. My coworkers, fellow trainees, were either cravenly opportunistic, practically drooling at the prospect of discovering a cash register to pilfer or scams to run in order to increase their bonuses, or were passive. None of what was going on could touch them. They were so in touch with themselves and so out of touch with the world outside that it never occurred to them that there might be something wrong.

When the Vice President of the West Coast division of Comcast stopped by to tell us that were lucky to work for a company that was only leveraged by a factor of seven to one, when he told us that with a 50% approval rating the Oregon Comcast office had the highest customer satisfaction rate in the country, and when he joked about CEO Brian Robert's personal problems, about how, in the old days, when Ralph was in charge, the kid kept losing millions of dollars from his personal fortune and kept having to be bailed out, we all basked in the glow of his insider's knowledge of the corruption. Everybody knew that they were participating in a con but they all thought they were wise.

Everyone who has been to the movies or maybe just rented a DVD knows that the confidence artist relies on the mark's own greed. You can't cheat an honest man. But while stealing a man's money requires inspiring his desire for a quick buck, the corporation needs more. The corporation needs your cynicism.

It is as though the Situationist critique of bureaucracy and work doesn't go far enough. The failure here is the failure to see how the identification of the good as something outside of work, outside of society, allows people to disavow the significance of the separation. The filmmaker Terrel Seltzer, whose film *Call it Sleep* is perhaps the only Situationist film in English, describes the problem for the spectator as one of false consciousness, but what he doesn't see is that the exposure of the lie, the removal of the curtain, can lead not to a liberated consciousness, but rather to a rejection of consciousness as intrinsically false.

It is not only cynicism, but the longing after what is good, not only false consciousness, but the stoic acceptance of the lie that was the real problem in the Comcast training room.

"I just don't want to end up like my father," Mike told me. "I'm using them."

And who was Mike's father? He was a born-again minister, but more than that his father was a man who had once sustained a brain injury and who'd spent ten years in a coma. Mike's father represented unconscious religiosity. And just what was the junky experience, if not just this kind of unconscious religiosity? What did it mean to be Comcastic if not to be sure of a goodness outside of life? How else any of us withstand the exposed con if not by secreting away our best selves as something that could never touch or be touched by the processes of power.

Simon's Unnatural Birth

On August 30th of 2003 we were all sitting at the foot of my wife's hospital bed and watching *Mister Roger's Neighborhood* on television. Cleansing sunlight streamed through the plate glass, reflecting off of the metal stand for the saline drip and the LED display of Simon's pulse rate. The sunlight made it difficult to make out just what precisely Fred Rogers was doing on the television screen. I knew that he was going to visit a gorilla who knew sign language, that he was going to meet an ape named Koko, but my eyelids were heavy, the picture on the screen was washed out, and I wasn't sure I was following the story properly. Still, from what I could tell Mister Rogers was sitting cross legged next to what looked to be a hole in the orange carpet, but when I opened my eyes wider I realized that what I'd taken to be a hole was in fact a figure—it was the signing ape named Koko.

Ben was next to me at the foot of the bed and he was awake with his Game Boy, while Miriam and Emma and Simon were napping above us. The saline solution was connected to my wife's arm, and the heart monitor was connected to my son Simon's foot.

Simon had arrived a month early and was just under six pounds. His Apgar score was a six, which was just on the cusp of normality, and everyone told us that there was no cause to worry, but the fact remained that Simon's arrival had not gone to plan. Miriam had intended to have a homebirth, and had been lucky to avoid an emergency C-section. The heart monitor counted out little beeps and everyone, all of us, breathed slowly and deeply in the afternoon sun. We were all finding the ground again after the terror of Miriam's 36 hours of labor.

"How do you say love in sign language?" Mister Rogers asked the gorilla's trainer and interpreter. Rather than teach Mister Rogers the sign the interpreter spoke for the gorilla.

"'What's that? Is that a flower?'" she asked for the gorilla. "She wants to know about your cufflinks," the trainer said.

"They are suns. My grandfather gave me these cufflinks."

I couldn't see Mister Rogers' expression but his voice sounded strained. He wanted to talk to this wonderful gorilla about love, but the gorilla was huge. The gorilla had grabbed Mister Rogers by his wrist and was reaching out for his cuff link with what might have been her tongue.

Simon's early arrival poked a hole in my understanding of how my life as a father was supposed to work out. While I understood intellectually that the due date the doctors and nurses had given us was just provisional, and while I knew that there were always unseen mechanical processes going on inside the body that could do unpredictable things, I nonetheless felt that these causes and processes would become known when through the effects they caused. What I was not prepared for was an intrusion or deviation, from the story that I'd been telling myself about birth life and death that could arrive without being knowable.

> "Lacan agrees with the German Idealist argument whereby any reference to 'external reality' falls short: our access to this 'reality' is always—already 'mediated' by the symbolic process. At this point, however, it is crucial to bear in mind the distinction between reality and the Real: the Real as 'impossible' is precisely the excess of 'immediacy' which cannot be 'reified' in a fetish, the unfathomable X which, although nowhere present, curves/

distorts any space of symbolic representation and condemns it to ultimate failure."[16]

What happened first was that her water broke and we were given about ten hours to come to some understanding of what this meant because while her water broke and she had some contractions there was nothing intense about the process. There was just a bit of fluid, not a gush that ran down her leg but hardly even changed the color of her denim pants, and every half an hour or so there was what Miriam described as a pinch.

While Miriam called her friends to her and alerted the midwifes I tried to recall what my job was supposed to be. I paced up and down the hall to our apartment, made a few pointless phone calls of my own, and then finally settled on the solution of a movie.

I watched Billy Wilder's film *The Apartment*, a film that is both a critique of capitalism and corporatism and justification of it. Jack Lemmon plays the part of a nameless drone in a Taylorist megacorporation, the kind of desk dweller who wears a suit to work, a nice red tie and a flower in his lapel, not because of any dress code but because he wants to make a good impression. He's the nice guy who is so eager to please that he lets people walk all over him, but he is also the cunning type who lets people take advantage of him but only if it will help him to get ahead.

Specifically Jack Lemmon lets his bosses use his apartment for their extramarital affairs, passing around the key to his home and even letting his supervisors kick him out of his own bed in the middle of the night, sleeping in the park, so that the executive might consummate his debauchery with his secretary.

Not to go too far down the road of the plot, the point of the movie was that the two main characters, Jack Lemmon's absurd little man and Shirley Maclaine's promiscuous elevator girl, are ultimately

16) Zizek, Slavoj, "Plague of Fantasies," London, Verson, 1997

redeemed by the harsh circumstances, the alienated and dishonest dealings, and the desperate and impoverished positions they find themselves in. They are disempowered workers who have no real integrity—he acts as a pimp and she like a whore—and yet they find each other precisely through this self-destruction. It is precisely when they act against convention that they truly come to be ethical, and there most ethical acts are also the most self destructive.

Consider just what it was that drove Shirley Maclaine to attempt suicide in the movie. She is having an affair with Fred McMurray, a man who she knows is married, but who is rich and powerful and who tells her all the things she wants to hear. Her suicide attempt does not come about when this powerful man rejects her or breaks off their relationship, but rather when a revelation about McMurray's philandering causes him to fall in her estimation. What is devastating is how thin and ignoble McMurray's desire is shown to be. It is much more devastating that a simple termination of the love affair would have been, but it is also much more liberating for Maclaine.

SHELDRAKE: I have a present for you. I didn't quite know what to get you—anyway it's a little awkward for me, shopping—(*he has taken out a money clip, detaches a bill*)—so here's a hundred dollars—go out and buy yourself something.

(*He holds the money out, but she doesn't move. Sheldrake slips the bill into her open bag.*)

SHELDRAKE: They have some nice alligator bags at Bergdorf's

(*Fran gets up slowly and starts peeling off her gloves. Sheldrake looks at her, then glances nervously at his wrist watch.*)

SHELDRAKE: Fran, it's a quarter to seven—and I mustn't miss the train— if we hadn't wasted all that time—I have to get home and trim the tree—

(*Fran has started to remove her coat.*)

FRAN: Okay. (*shrugs the coat back on*) I just thought as long as it was paid
    for—

SHELDRAKE: (*an angry step toward her*) Don't ever talk like that, Fran!
    Don't make yourself out to be cheap.

FRAN: A hundred dollars? I wouldn't call that cheap …

It is after this that Maclaine's character tries to kill herself with
sleeping pills. The question is why?

My memories fit together into this question about why it should
be that Koko the gorilla, Maclaine's liberation from *The Apartment*,
my son's birth, or the recognition of the contingency of physical
reality itself should be traumatizing. In each case what seems to be
presenting itself is a kind of impossibility, or incongruity. There is
something that doesn't fit, something disrupts the usual frame of
reference, in each case:

Koko was not a mildly stunted human, but a real gorilla. Simon's
birth was not a natural harmonious moment but an intrusive
physical event. Fred MacMurray wasn't an exceptional romantic,
but a brutal philanderer.

And when enough of these ruptures or failures stack up one starts
to suspect the legitimacy of the whole system. The very space or
substance which supports your illusions starts to give way.

Ideology and Mister Rogers

In Raoul Vanegeim's 1967 book, *The Revolution of Everyday Life*, he describes the way ideology functions in a disintegrating world, the reason so many continue to support institutions they hate, work jobs that are stultifying, and lead lives of quiet desperation. We are, he says, like Wile E. Coyote in a Warner Brothers cartoon. That is we have run over the edge of the cliff, we are hanging in air, but we don't realize it yet. That is, while we may subjectively know that global warming is an apocalyptic threat, or that the internal contradictions in the economy are threatening a global depression, or that the death of the institutions of liberal bourgeois democracy is certain to bring on authoritarian regimes, we continue to objectively believe that the world is stable, that capitalism and America are forever, and that our 15 minutes are just around the next corner. The problem is that we are looking for our beliefs in all the wrong places. Our beliefs aren't to be found in our private thoughts, or the fashionable wrappings of our everyday lives. Our beliefs are to be found in our daily practices, in the habits and rituals that fill our days.

> "As cynical subjects we know full well that our understanding of reality is distorted, but we nevertheless stick to that falsehood and do not reject it. Instead of Marx's formula for ideology, then—'they do not know it, but they are doing it,' Sloterdijk proposes a cynical variation on it—'they know very well what they are doing, but still, they are doing it...'"[17]

17) *Myers, Tony. "Slavoj Zizek". New York, Routledge, 2003*

64

Tony Myers points out in his book that Marx's critique of money, Marx's assertion that money is materially worthless and functions only as a symbol for social relations and inequality, is well known.

> "Individuals already know that money itself is not valuable. They are completely aware in their day—to—day use of money that it is only an indirect expression of wealth ... Nevertheless people act as if money were inherently valuable." [18]

There are hundreds of examples of ideology in practice, an ideology that functions despite cynicism, or that is perhaps even supported by such cynicism. Belief in Santa Claus, for example, does not require that the parents or children really believe, but only that the stockings are stuffed with candy and cheap toys from China. The holy rite of Communion is another example. The participant in this ritual is not required to literally believe or experience the bread and wine on offer as literally transformed into the body of and blood of Christ—rather it is the act of consuming the wafer that is the act of transubstantiation. If one were to actually experience the wafer as a piece of human flesh this would amount to experiencing a delusion. It would perhaps, from a religious perspective, be evidence of demonic possession.

The ritual does your experiencing for you.

Another example of ideology in action would be viewing a children's program such as *Mister Roger's Neighborhood* on television. Here we participate in the fiction of parenting and childhood as an enlightenment project of self discovery. "Mister Rogers encourages parents, grandparents and teachers to cherish the questions and comments that come from their children."

While we watch the reruns from Roger's neighborhood we might experience the program as an empty charade from a soft-spoken if not somewhat fruity, spokesperson of public television,

---

18) Myers, Tony. *"Slavoj Zizek"*. *New York, Routledge, 2003*

a representative of upper-middle-class middle-brow bourgeois democracy, the program itself acts out a belief in dialogue, imagination, childhood, nurturing care, and community.

The program is chockfull of rituals. Mister Rogers removes his jacket and leather shoes and replaces these items with a zip up sweater and a pair of comfy tennis shoes. Mister Rogers feeds his fish, he visits Picture/Picture, and sends his model Trolley through the fourth wall and into the neighborhood of make-believe.

In order to fully appreciate the ideological function, it's helpful to remember that Mister Rogers was both a psychologist and Presbyterian minister. That is he was not an innocent or naive creator of unconscious ideologies but constructed his message with intention. The program did not reflect the dominant values of television but instead worked to subvert those values and offer another set of values and offer another set of values to be acted out in a new neighborhood and when ideology is no longer conceived as a set of false beliefs, but rather as a form of collective behavior. When ideology is materialized the cognition or exposure of an ideology as an ideology ceases to be the end goal of a critique, but rather can be seen as the starting point.

> Dear Mister Rogers,
>
> Are you real? Are you under a mask or costume like Big Bird? Are you for real or not? My birthday wish is I want to know if you are for real.
>
> From Timmy, age 5

•

> Dear Timmy,
>
> ... That's a good question. It's hard for children to understand what they see on television. I'm glad that you are a person who wonders about things and that you ask questions about what you're wondering. Asking questions is a good way to grow and learn!

You asked if I am a real person. I am a real person, just the way you are a real person. Your television set is a special way that you can see the picture of me and hear my voice. I can't look out through the television set to see or hear my television friends, but I think about them whenever we make our television visits.[19]

So what is ideology of Mister Rogers Neighborhood, and how does it function in practice?

To sum it up with just a few big words, the neighborhood is ontologically materialist, epistemologically realist, and politically a mixture of bourgeois democracy and socialism. The neighborhood was built to reflect these values—it was a televisual space filled in with these ideas.

Mister Rogers was first and foremost an advocate for children's educational television. A psychologist and a minister, Mister Rogers was not a proponent of a vision of childhood as an Eden-like state of extreme vulnerability and inner conflict. Children, from Fred Rogers' way of thinking, are creatures born too soon, small, and defenseless, and arrive with drives, impulses, and predilections that try to overwhelm them. Far from needing protection from the adult world, children require emotional and intellectual instruction from adults, they need adults, they need adult help to learn the difference between thoughts and objects and right and wrong.

Mister Rogers saw childhood through a Freudian lens, the lessons he broadcast to his television neighbors were always aimed at helping children to discover ways to sublimate their libidinal impulses, to manage their fears, and to develop a domesticated imaginal realm. He aimed to teach children how to safely express their emotions through music or other creative expressive techniques, he looked upon playtime as a space wherein children do the work of growing up, and he was always quick to point out that open communications, especially with adults or other elders or

19) Rogers, Fred. "Dear Mister Rogers," Penguin Books, New York, 1996

authorities, was essential for children who were making their way into the world.

Compare Fred Rogers to Willy Wonka. While both men act as gatekeepers and guides into a realm of imagination, their tone and techniques are totally opposed. While Wonka escorts the children onto a steamboat and takes them through a Tunnel of Love in his own factory, a nightmare realm where filmed images of beheaded chickens, green faces, centipedes, lava lamps, and villains wearing top hats. Wonka's is a ritual meant to be taken as reality. Mister Rogers on the other hand, asks the children to allow his mechanical trolley to take the journey for them. The passage from reality to the Neighborhood of Make-Believe is accompanied with chimes and the sound of the trolley moving down the tracks.

Dear Mister Rogers,

Why do you use a trolley?

Kevin, age 11

•

Dear Kevin,

There are a couple of reasons for that. First of all, we wanted to have a way of separating our Neighborhood (where things happen in a real way) from Make—Believe (where things can happen by pretending or by magic). Secondly, we wanted to show that we could all go together to another place—the Neighborhood of Make Believe—by pretending.[20]

Mister Rogers even showed us where the Trolley's controls were hidden because he thought it was "important to show that trolleys don't operate independently of people. It was important to emphasize that its people who make machines work. I think its healthy to demystify this medium of television as much as we can."[21]

---

20) Rogers, Fred. "Dear Mister Rogers," Penguin Books, New York, 1996
21) IBID

This emphasis on realism, on demystifying life and its operations, is essential to Rogers' mission. He is always asking the same question of the musicians, basketball players, actors, mailmen, and others who visit him in his television house.

"What were you like as a child. How did you come to be good at what you do? Who taught you, influenced you?"

When visiting a pretzel factory, or an assembly line for electric cars, he always asked the workers how they did it, how long each step in production took, and how they came to be so good at what they did. Rogers' motto is that people do things—that pretzels and violins and Twinkies don't come into the world on their own.

Rogers' message is that people are special individually, that they aren't to be treated as means but as ends, and that people can make things. People are the only agents of production in Roger's universe.

> "Zizek argues that the typical postmodern subject in one who displays an outright cynicism toward official institutions, yet at the same time firmly believes in the existence of conspiracies and an unseen Other pulling the strings. This apparently contradictory coupling of cynicism and belief is strictly correlative to the demise of the big Other. You therefore display cynicism and belief in equal measures."[22]

While it is true that Mister Rogers is a humanist, a realist, an educator, it is also true that his is a normative education. He aims at orienting children in the world and not at disorienting adults. Mister Rogers believes in people, people are the ones who do things, but in Roger's neighborhood there are no divisions between people. No capitalists and workers, no rich and poor.

That is, while Mister Rogers is glad to show the controls for his trolley, glad to expose the real mechanism behind his Neighborhood of Make Believe, the project of exposing the magical or make

---

22) Myers, Tony. "Slavoj Zizek". Routledge, New York. 2003, pg 57

believe mechanisms that control what is real in the neighborhood is well beyond his mission.

Consider: Mister Rogers takes off his shoes and dress coat when he walks in his television house. He performs a ritual that believes in the natural rightness of the division between work and leisure, a ritual that performs this belief so we no longer are required to believe anything. He talks to the factory worker and factory owner with the same kind of magnanimous tone of voice. And the puppet King in the neighborhood is only a bumbling narcissist and not an enemy of democracy and liberty.

> "How could one carry on the class struggle on the basis of the philosophical Thesis: 'it is man who makes history'? It might be said that this Thesis is useful in fighting against a certain conception of 'History': history in submission to the decisions of a Deity or to the Ends of Providence. But, speaking seriously, that is no longer the problem!"[23]

Mister Rogers was a television personality, a psychologist, a minister. He spoke kindly and presented the best aspects of today's ruling ideology. After all, who isn't afraid of Santa Claus, who isn't glad to know that one can't go down the drain or get flushed down the toilet? Who isn't relieved to hear that those machines aren't independent of us, that we humans are really in charge despite appearances to the contrary?

Mister Rogers was a decent man, a good neighbor, but like much else in today's world of hidden ideologies, his message is begging to be detourned, derailed, or simply toppled.

---

23) *Althusser, Louis. "On Ideology" Graham Lock Trans., Verso, London, 1972*

Economic Collapse

Looking out at the sloped concrete on the underside of the I-5 overpass, waiting behind a Plexiglas window in a light rail train, staring out at the anonymous people disembarking at the Rose Quarter Transit Center. I listened to my iPod, to the conspiracy shock jock Alex Jones, and considered the hidden forces at work in my life. I looked out the train window at the people out there on the other side—at a sloppy man who wiped his nose with his hand and then used it to adjust his bushy beard, at a neat and tidy older man in a beige jacket whose gray hair was the same color as the plastic frames of his glasses, at an obese woman in an oversized leather vest whose tennis shoes were laced loosely in order to accommodate her abundant feet—did any of them realize that they were living through the collapse of civilization?

Lehman Brothers had failed and President Bush had announced a commitment to "act to strengthen and stabilize US financial markets and improve investor confidence" which, as far as I could tell, amounted to a promise to hand the debt to people like those of us who were commuting to work.

I stared blankly at the slogans written in spray paint outside my window. I read "Down with the Abyss," and "Too many hipsters not enough Crime," and wondered if the Comcast cubicle farm would remain open for very much longer. Credit markets were frozen and the President was doing his Bambi impression again. He told us that he had a plan, but all the while he did that same blinking routine he'd perfected eight years earlier when he'd announced his open cheat as a legitimate victory.

I knew that capitalism was in crisis, but the screaming rant from my iPod's ear buds made me feel better. Listening to Alex Jones made sense, even when nothing else did. None of the liberal alternatives—*Democracy Now, This American Life, Car Talk*—seemed to connect. Amy Goodman cleared her throat, Ira Glass whined, and Tom and Ray explained how to change the oil in a 1976 Dodge Dart, whereas Alex Jones sounded like he was awake as he explained how the credit crisis had been planned in advance. It was all a controlled demolition, and just like the last controlled demolition it involved using exotic weapons and instruments like CDOs in the service of a psychological attack on the US public. The crisis was staged in order to create the conditions necessary to impose a totalitarian regime on the people. It was simply the most current actualization of a long term plan to create a "Prison Planet," and while Jones foamed at the mouth and fell into hysterical mock laughter, while he began to sound more and more insane, the story he told sounded more and more plausible. Looking out at the cement walls of the overpass, counting the umbrellas and blank stares amongst the throngs waiting on the platform, it felt as though nothing could ever change. That even as the conspiracy unwound, even as the economy came to a grinding halt, it did so in service of a sameness that seemed all pervasive.

Minutes later we entered the Robertson tunnel and the Max train slowed under the west hills. We stopped underground, and I looked out again. I looked out at the Washington Park Max Station, at the curved metal mesh overhead, at the Lite Brite postmodern cave paintings that had been commissioned by the city, at the uneven granite stools, and at the drilling sample. There was a geological timeline in a tube of glass, history presented as a matter of sedimentation, and crisis became real.

Alex Jones expressed my anger with the system in a way that I could secretly enjoy, but looking at the core of time—this condensed detritus and inorganic sediment, this catastrophe that was time and life—the crisis took on a dimension that I could no longer enjoy. I felt like I'd been erased, or that I could be erased. The economic collapse felt like an awakening, a self-awareness that I was myself already fossilized, just a bit of sediment.

As the train pulled away from the underground station I involuntarily remembered a British cartoon program that played on PBS in the early seventies, a show called *Simon in the Land of Chalk Drawings*. The premise of the show was that a little boy named Simon had discovered some magic chalk that gave him the power to bring all of his drawings to life, and to live in the spaces he himself drew. Each week the boy would find a limestone wall or an empty bit of sidewalk on his way to school. The show consisted of the lands, stick figure friends, and adventures that Simon created for himself out of chalk.

On my way to work that morning I felt a little like I was a chalk drawing myself. Maybe there really was a conspiracy, maybe there really was a controller, but if so the puppet master was more likely to be a British animator working out a game of Simon Says than a banker or Bildeberger. And while Alex Jones and others ranted and shouted for Simon's head, another option was open to all of the drawings. We might try to get our hands on the chalk.

The Dream of a Snow Day

When I was in grade school in Colorado I would frequently long for snow, and while I enjoyed playing in it (sledding, skiing, starting snowball fights, laying down in it to make snow angels) the real attraction was how snow promised to stop the world. I wasn't alone in my desire. Everyone, all of my classmates, felt the same way. When the weatherman would point to blue triangles on the weather map, point to curved blue lines with spikes that indicated cold fronts or point to cartoon snowflakes, we would all stay up late and watch the sky from our warm bedrooms. Snow meant we would escape the humdrum routine of school life, that homework could remain unfinished. Freedom was frozen and fell from the sky, and it might just fall down on us if we kept a light on in the window.

After Lehman Brothers collapsed I felt the same way about economic collapse as I had felt about snow in grade school. What if I turned up at work and found the doors closed, maybe padlocked. My tedious life as a cubicle worker would be disrupted.

The desire for disruption did not conflict with the outrage I felt; it was not a counterbalance to my fear, but was supported by the fear. This was the other reason that Alex Jones was compelling. If it turned out that American workers were going to be dispossessed of their meager possessions, their jobs, their ticky tacky homes, then there was a chance that life might turn out to be an adventure after all.

"One can conceive each big break in the history of the West as a kind of 'unplugging.' The Greek philosophical wondering 'unplugs' from the immersion into the mythical universe; Judaism 'unplugs' from the polytheistic jouissance; Christianity 'unplugs' from one's substantial community. The big question here is: how are these three unpluggings interrelated?"[24]

Unlike when I was child, when both my physical self and imagination were smaller, what I hoped for upon reading about and watching the financial crisis was not for the collapse to occur within my everyday life, but for the collapse of my everyday life. This was my fantasy. Despite what seemed like an eternal present peopled with video images, soup labels, detergents, and the slow decay of time's passage, there was still a chance that history might start up again.

When I found the Comcast call center open, when the rows of carpeted walls and the staccato of repeated pitches for telephonic highspeed television greeted me, I felt even more despair.

I had to work, there had been no collapse, but it was manifesting as a continuation of the long pitch for HBO and The Playboy Channel.

I made my way to my desk and put my headset on, waited for my HP desktop computer to boot, and remembered how the neutron bomb was supposed to work. When a neutron bomb exploded all the buildings remained standing but all biological life burned away. The financial collapse worked the same way. All of the rituals and practices of the capitalist system would remain intact, but the living dream that supported capitalism had burned away.

A long high pitch beep sounded in my left ear. "It's a terrific day at Comcast, how can I help you?"

Walt, the forty-something man in the cubicle next to mine, took off his headset. "I can't imagine myself working here for 20 years or

24) *Zizek, Slavoj. "On Belief" Routledge, New York, 2001*

even ten years. Just can't picture it," he told me.

"What would you do if they fired you?" I asked.

"I have no idea," he said. "Something else."

"What if money wasn't a problem? What would you do then? What would you want to do?"

"If money wasn't a problem?"

"Would you just stay at home?"

"With my wife and her kid? No, thank you," he said.

Another call came in and I explained how the offers available online were not the same as the offers we were authorized to make over the phone. I tried to sell the 20-year-old girl who had called for internet a package that included phone service as well. When she wouldn't bite on that I let her walk without selling her anything because a sale without phone service would hurt my metrics more than a call without any sale at all.

"What would you do if you were fired?" Walt asked. And I realized that I didn't have a satisfactory answer to the question either. It seemed to demand that I say something more than golf or mow the lawn. Not having to work offered up a challenge. What was worth doing for its own sake?

"I'd walk," I said.

"Walk?"

"Like Forrest Gump, you know? Just walk in a straight line for as long as I could."

"Forrest Gump ran."

Blue Beam Conspiracy

The trouble with Alex Jones and all the other advocates of paranoid awareness, all the other enemies of the control system, is that none of them are quite paranoid enough to understand what's going on. A prime example of the difficulty would be how various conspiracy investigators have dealt with the Blue Beam Theory.

What is Project Blue Beam? My friend, Neil Kramer, summed it up in his blog, The Cleaver, this way: "In short, Project Blue Beam is a highly classified black-budget project that takes the application of holographic technology to another level. An integrated array of satellite-mounted lasers and ground installations will be used to simulate large-scale religious manifestations and a hostile alien presence. Gods, messiahs, extra terrestrials, motherships—the whole shooting match. Truly a show to capture the imagination."

What's going on then is that the government (the real government mind you, not the puppets you see on television) is planning to stage a phony UFO event in order to foist a new religion onto the public and gain complete control of the population. Still, what's most interesting about the Blue Beam story is that those who take it seriously are actually convinced that real UFO landings have already occurred. The late William Cooper, for example, was convinced that the government had made a secret pact with ETs, an agreement to allow the aliens to abduct humans in exchange for alien technology. He also believed that sometime after 2010 the government would stage a UFO landing on the White House lawn in order to brainwash the public that aliens were real and that they were wise, lovable, and altogether superior. In fact, Cooper thought that the government would use alien technology in order to pull off the fake UFO stunt, and that the aliens themselves were giving the orders. That is, the big secret was that the fake UFO landing would in fact be orchestrated by real aliens. This was a fraud that has to be true in order to fool anyone, or a truth that could only be presented as a lie.

If one stops to consider the story it quickly takes on its contradiction. Whatever remains convincing about the Blue Beam conspiracy theory stems only from the deadlock. The possibility that Blue Beam could be true in any conventional or empirical way dissolves, but we are left with the contradiction at its core. And to continue we have to adopt a sort of dream logic.

What is truly strange about the Blue Beam scenario is the way in which this deadlock, this self-contradiction, seems to be endemic not just to conspiracy theories, but also to philosophical systems of epistemology and ontology.

For example, Bishop George Berkeley posited that the world was made entirely of perception. He demonstrated that what we take to be matter, that abstract substance without qualities that provided a substrate for perceived reality, was nothing more than a category mistake. Matter itself was logically impossible. How could something be if it had no way of being? How could something without any perceptible qualities be the source of all perceptions? What Berkeley proved was that the matter, in order to be the substrate that supported reality, also had to cease to exist. A substance without qualities, an essence without expression, this was what matter had to be, and as such matter could not be.

The trouble was, that by eliminating matter, Berkeley also exposed at least a methodology for eliminating any and all other substrates.

Attempts were made to correct the problem, but in every case the contradiction would reappear. Kant's synthetic apriori truth, being a contingent proof that was also necessary, is the first example that comes to mind. But there are others.

And if one leaves philosophy behind, if one moves into religion or spirituality, for instance, the impasse is only ignored, but it doesn't disappear. In religion we have Christ who is both God and man at the same time. Or we have Zen with its universal mind that is also no mind.

When one sees this contradiction, this split between reality and what is perceived popping up everywhere, the temptation is to attempt to reconcile the contradiction by blending the two into one. To put it in terms of Blue Beam, this amounts to believing the conspiracy.

Yes the aliens are among us, but they are also really a cover story for some other deeper mystery. In the case of philosophy this means abandoning the questions of ontology and epistemology and caring only about utilitarian questions. In religion it means believing in God on Sundays, or it means accepting that neither our perceptions of the world nor our ideas about what lies behind the world are worth a damn. Instead one adapts methods, breathing methods, thinking methods, to help one remain unattached and uninvolved. With this approach we go along to get along, adopt a tolerance toward everything, meditate, and eat lots of bran.

But what this misses is that Blue Beam is a symptom. That it is itself imbalanced. The conspiracy theory itself is the conspiracy, and on that level, right on the surface, it is a conspiracy that can be unwound, or figured out.

In December 2009 I discussed project Blue Beam with the blogger and mystic Neil Kramer:

"These inorganic beings who are putting forward memes like Blue Beam or this new movie about 2012 ... isn't there a risk involved in that? For instance, if the Blue Beam conspiracy were to happen, that could be an event that would disrupt the day to day grind significantly. I would think that it would be profoundly disruptive to believe the Earth was being attacked by aliens ... isn't there always a risk to one of these psy-ops?"

His reply was interesting.

"I think the risks are very, very carefully calculated. So that there is practically zero percent chance of anything going wrong. Take the Revelation of the Method principle. It's a technique of trauma programming whereby the dominance of the controller over the subject is amplified through the disclosure of their own control and this increases the submission. They show the unconscious how profoundly effected you are by how they control you. And there is nothing you can do about it. And you consent to it. You continue to give your power to this machine."

Listening to Neil talk, even as I understood that he was attempting to bring a positive message, I felt trapped.

Project Blue Beam, stories of space beams destroying the Trade Center towers, the notion of the Revelation of Method, what these conspiracy stories have in common is that the are all, at base, fatalist. The conspiracy is large. It's older than Western Civilization. There are Galactic forces at work. In fact, it's likely that the conspiracy is embedded into the fabric of reality itself.

Whatever the story, however grand the scale, the effect is always the same. This is the Revelation of the Method, and it's easy to see how it can lead to a fatalistic attitude.

But perhaps what is less easy to see is just what this fatalism is and how it functions.

In Richard Taylor's 1962 short philosophy book, *Metaphysics*, he put forward a story and argument for fatalism as a coherent, and indeed necessary, philosophical position. Taylor told the story of a young Hoosier librarian with a chronic ulcer. This was the story of Osmo.

It began with a scribe who heard the voice of God. God said, "He of whom I speak is the one called Osmo." And in this way over the course of many days God told the scribe one mind numbing detail about Osmo after another, and the scribe, knowing his job, wrote all the details down. When the voice stopped the scribe collected all that he'd written and sought a way to publish the facts as a book.

> "He at first gave it the title *The Life of Osmo, as Given by God*, but thinking that people would take this to be some sort of joke, he dropped the reference to God."[25]

The *Life of Osmo* was not a popular book, in fact many thought that it was quite a strange book as it didn't have a story but was merely a collection of unrelated facts about a very ordinary person. Very few people purchased copies, very few libraries carried it, however one copy of *The Life of Osmo* was purchased by a library and this copy collected dust for many years until a librarian in Indiana, a librarian named Osmo, discovered it there.

Osmo was quite shocked to find the book at first, and then he became quite obsessed by it. He spent an afternoon reading about his life. The first few chapters convinced him that the book was accurate, but as he approached the end of the book his opinion of the work turned. He decided that the volume was ultimately unsatisfying. For one thing, the book was tedious, and for another it was far too short.

What was really disturbing was that the Osmo in the book died in a plane crash during a flight to Idaho during his 28th year. Osmo

---

25) Taylor, Richard. "Metaphysics" Prentice-Hall, Inc., New Jersey, 1962

the librarian was terrified by this detail, and he committed to forego any possible plane trip to Idaho.

Ultimately, Taylor explains, Osmo died just as God predicted. During a flight to Portland, Osmo panicked when his flight was waylaid by inclement weather and rerouted to Boise. Osmo's very panic was what brought the plane down.

What happens after Osmo finds a book full of true statements about his future?

> "Osmo's extraordinary circumstances led him to embrace the doctrine of fatalism. Not quite completely, perhaps, for there he was right up to the end, trying vainly to buck his fate—trying, in effect, to make a fool of God, though he did not know this, because he had no idea of the book's source."[26]

One might think that taking a fatalistic perspective on life would lead one to suicide, or at least to passivity, but that is not how it works. The idea of destiny, the concept that the future is full of truth, claims that could conceivably be known now, and that regardless of whether they are known or not, demonstrate conclusively that there can only be one possible future and not another, the idea of fate, doesn't work as a brake on action, but rather motivates the fatalist to continue on with his useless struggle.

> "Shall we (the fatalists) sit idly by, passively observing the changing scene without participation, never testing our strength and our goodness, having no hand in what happens, or in making things come out as they should? This is a question for which each will find his own answer. Some men do little or nothing with their lives, and might as well never have lived, they make such a waste of it. Others do much, and the lives of a few even shine like the stars."[27]

In the above quote we find that even a pure, arid, and godless

---

26) Taylor, Richard. "Metaphysics" Prentice-Hall, Inc., New Jersey, 1962.
27) IBID

fatalism inevitably leads to a kind of Calvinism. Taylor's description of how some men are idle and some active, some burn bright and some are dim, is nothing but a recapitulation of the doctrine of divine grace. If one wants to be close to God, if one wants to be among the chosen, there is nothing to do but wait and judge. That is, only by your own acts will you be able to determine what your spiritual nature was predetermined by God to actually be.

In the Blue Beam Theory the US government is planning to stage a phony UFO event in order to foist a new religion onto the public and gain complete control of the population. 9/11 was a false flag attack meant to get everyone to accept the illegal invasions of Afghanistan and Iraq. Lifting a detail from the 9/11 conspiracy, the anthrax attacks were staged in order to spread panic after the attacks in September and to create a pretext for blaming Iraq. Operation Gladio was the code name for a NATO "stay-behind" operation in Italy that implemented a strategy of tension, including false flag attacks, in order to stave off the threat of Communism after World War II. Gladio was behind, for example, the Peteano massacre of 1972, a NATO-sanctioned act of terrorism that was originally blamed on the Red Brigades.

Regardless of whether the conspiracy theory is absurd or possible, regardless of whether the story is based on rock solid evidence or pure conjecture, the structure of the story is often the same. The conspiracist tells us that history is staged for us. Your government concocts reasons for its policies based on pseudo events and false flag attacks. Further, once you accept the reality of the conspiracy you find it impossible to view your government in the same way as before. What was once your government is now no longer yours at all. Once the reality of Blue Beam is digested the most pressing question becomes: Who are the others?

The conspiracy offers various answers. The others are the Bildebergers, or they are the people who work on the Trilateral

Commission. Perhaps the others are Galactic oversouls who have been manipulating the Earth for generations. But, whoever they are said to be, these others always function as Jews. That is, the others are always a group who stand in for the inconsistency, the contradiction, in society. Life is out of balance, the center doesn't hold, and the more obvious the failure becomes the more necessary an imagined other becomes. There must be someone who is consistent, someone who is whole, somebody who knows.

Again, the problem with conspiracy theorists is that they aren't paranoid enough. The truth is that fatalism lends support to unexamined attachments to the heroic free subject. The Blue Beam conspiracy of a phony UFO landing props up the story of secret alien contact. The relentless pursuit of evidence of US complicity in the attacks of 9/11 can prop up a belief that the US republic is the best of all possible political systems. Anti-semitic attacks on Jews as the inauthentic, homeless, neurotic, insidious, masters of the conspiracy that is modern life props up a faith in the logic of dispossession, inauthenticity, and neurosis that defines modern life.

Taylor posits that there is a set of truth claims about the past, and it is logically impossible for the past not to correlate with the set of truth claims that exist to describe it. That is, while we can imagine that Lee Harvey Oswald did not act alone, that there was a conspiracy behind JFK's assassination, we cannot imagine that a truth statement like "Lee Harvey Oswald acted alone" can retain its status as a truth claim unless Lee Harvey Oswald acted alone. Revisionists don't require Time Machines.

Taylor's next step is simply to apply this understanding of truth claims to future events. He says that there is a set of truth claims about the future, and the future therefore must correlate with this as yet undiscovered set of truth claims.

The problem is not in the logically coherent and necessary correlation between a set of truth claims about the future and the future itself, but in the presupposition of the truth claims.

The French psychoanalyst Jacques Lacan argued that it was always impossible to state the entirety of what was true. His argument can be considered as a version of Zeno's paradox. That is, any given true statement will run up against an infinite regress if it attempts to justify its truth with other truth statements. You set off to prove that Lee Harvey Oswald acted alone and you discover an infinite number of claims, of truth statements, even when you're just describing his arrival at the book depository. Oswald's relationship with the FBI, his relationship with his wife, his possible friendship with Jack Ruby, all of these are factors that create their own sets of truth claims. It's a mystery wrapped in a riddle inside an enigma.

Any set of truth claims that correlates with the totality of a past or future event would have to be an infinite set. Therefore any such set of truths about an event would be impossible to utter. Taylor argues that his fatalism doesn't rely on God in order to work, but since every set of truth claims for an event are necessarily inaccessible, since they constitutionally cannot be expressed as a totality, it seems obvious that the existence of such a set of claims relies on the positing of one who knows the set. And only God could accomplish the sort of knowing required.

Without this God the possibility that an infinite set of truth claims could exist is reduced to nothing. And without such a set of truth claims we are placed in the awkward position of having to simply decide.

Did Lee Harvey Oswald act alone? Was he a victim of the CIA mind control program MKULTRA? What planet was he from? Did Oswald kill Kennedy or did Kennedy stage his own assassination in order to entrap Oswald? Not all answers to these questions are of equal value. Some of the questions themselves are ridiculous, but without a set of hypothetical truth claims known in advance by God we can only subjectively arrive at our conclusions.

Every conclusion becomes an act of creation.

But, let us be clear. This does not mean that we are the source of our perceptions, the deciders of Real events. Rather this means that we are the aliens who stage fake UFO landings. We are the Jews, the disharmony, the gap. Ultimately we are the center that doesn't hold. And that is a terrible responsibility.

Simon and the Balloon

In December 2009, I scheduled 10 days off work. One of the perks of working for a large corporation was that I could take up to two weeks and still get paid. I anticipated receiving notes on a rewrite of a novel, a book that I'd sold to a New York publisher, and I'd use my vacation time to rewrite everything to the specifications of my editor. For me the last month of the zero years included 10 blank days, and I hoped I could use those empty spaces on the calendar to rewrite my ticket out of the everyday grind I'd found myself in, but then the editors notes didn't arrive.

"I know, I know. I'm killing you. I'm sorry," my editor said when I got him on the phone.

Still, rather than cancel my vacation, I took them. I didn't go anywhere, didn't plan on doing anything particularly.

According to the philosopher Henri Lefebvre space is never neutral or merely empty, but is always appears in a particular form or shape:

> "Specialized works keep their audience abreast of all sorts of equally specialized spaces: leisure, work, play, transportation, public facilities—all are spoke of in spatial terms."[28]

Guy Debord tells us that time is also never neutral. In his *Society of the Spectacle* he outlines the various shapes of time. There is the

28) Lefebvre, Henri. *"The Production of Space,"* Donald Nicholson-Smith Trans. *Blackwell Publishing, Malden, 1991*

circle of prehistoric time, the line of history, and the square block of an historical time that is frozen and separated from people.

Those ten days appeared to me as a home I never really wanted: my 60s style ranch house with a lime green trim. I had nowhere to go and no agenda, and so I mulled over the fact of this life that I hadn't really chosen, and insisted that we all watch old *Doctor Who* episodes from the 70s. Watching a bohemian time traveler face off against killer robots that looked like nothing other than upturned trashcans made me feel somewhat better.

Three days into this unproductive break was a payday, and while I had no desire to return to Beaverton, while I was enjoying the quiet of my alienation, I had to go back in to work to fetch my paycheck. As I found my coat and the door, Simon insisted on coming along.

"What if you had never married Mama?" he asked. We were at the stop on 60th and Interstate 84, surrounded by concrete and the sound of traffic passing. The sound of the combustion engines inside green station wagons and red sports cars made it impossible to hear so I had to wait until we were inside the train car, sitting in our orange bucket seats, to ask him to say it again.

"What if you'd never married Mama," Simon asked. He was a skinny little boy, six years old, with 70s style Beatles hair that we thought looked so cute on him. He looked sincerely concerned.

"If I hadn't married your mother? I'd miss you guys I suppose. I wouldn't have you, would I?"

"You'd miss me?" Simon smiled at this but his eyes seemed to harden and his giggle seemed a bit forced. "No, you wouldn't miss me. I would never have been born."

One of the signs above Simon's head explained that there were security cameras on the train, and the next one to that exhibited a poem. It was part of a city's arts program called Poetry in Motion.

The poem was entitled "Language Exists because ..." and the first line read:

"Language exists because nothing exists between those who express themselves."

Simon looked out the window, he glanced up at the sky and I wondered if he looked like me. I tried to conjure up memories of the Polaroid photo album my parents had kept, tried to recall if I'd ever looked as confident and yet disconnected. Simon was dressed in a red turtleneck and brown khaki pants. He was wearing blue Keds. Miriam and I had done the best we could to recreate remembered childhood fashions, but did Simon really look like me?

> "Fixated on the delusory center around which his world seems to move, the spectator no longer experiences life as a journey toward fulfillment and toward death. Once he has given up on really living he can no longer acknowledge his own death. Life insurance ads merely insinuate that he may be guilty of dying without having provided for the smooth continuation of the system following the resultant economic loss... On all the other fronts of advertising bombardment it is strictly forbidden to grow old. Everybody is urged to economize on their "youth—capital," though such capital, however carefully managed, has little prospect of attaining the durable and cumulative properties of economic capital. This social absence of death coincides with the social absence of life."[29]

Arriving at Comcast, Simon enjoyed traveling between cubicle walls. He laughed when he discover a cardboard cut-out of Spiderman, of Homer Simpson, and of Darth Vader, while I felt an urge to get through the rat maze as quickly as possible. We'd get the cheese (my paycheck) and get out.

I found myself dreading the prospect of introducing my son to my

---

29) Debord, Guy, "Society of the Spectacle", Ken Knabb Trans., Bureau of Public Secrets, www.bopsecrets.org, 2002.

bosses, and when we reached the pod of cubicles where I worked my feeling of agedness became more profound. I was proud of Simon, glad to see that my colleagues were charmed by his manner and the easy way he made demands on them (his naive egoism was his winningest characteristic) but I was also embarrassed to be who I was, to be a father and not a child.

"You still don't have electronic deposit set up?" The assistant manager asked me as he opened his desk drawer produced my paycheck.

"No. I'm a Luddite."

"You should get electronic deposit. If you'd had set that up then you wouldn't have had to come in for this during your vacation."

"I still use a VCR," I said.

Simon looked inside the manager's desk drawer and then gestured for me to come to him. I leaned over so he could whisper in my ear.

"Do you have some candy in your desk drawer?" I asked the manager.

"Jolly Ranchers. They're prizes. I give them out to top sellers. That's why you don't know about them already."

"Do you think …"

The assistant manager opened the drawer and Simon reached in and grabbed a handful.

"Just one," the manager said.

Simon stood there next to the desk and examined the pile he had. He held up the a piece to my manager.

"What's this one?"

"The green one? That's apple."

"That's good, right. Take that one," I said.

"What's this?" Simon asked.

"The red one?"

"That's cherry. Take cherry," I said.

"That's watermelon actually," the assistant manager said.

"Watermelon?" Simon asked.

"Yes."

Simon dropped the rest of the candy back into the desk drawer and then unwrapped the watermelon-flavored Jolly Rancher. He popped the hard candy into his mouth, and handed me the wrapper.

If I'd been asked to pick a flavor myself I would have also picked watermelon or some other flavor with a stinging aftertaste. My life was doubled or tripled upon itself. There was a point of view problem. I wasn't seeing anything directly, but everything came to me through a haze of concepts and feeling. I was seeing the cubicle walls from four feet off the ground, imagining the impact of the trip to my father's workplace on my young psyche. I was looking at the employee and his young son from my position behind my metal desk. I imagined what it would be like to view the scene from across the aisle. What would one of Craig's teammates think of me in this moment?

> "The spectacle obliterates the boundaries between self and world by crushing the self besieged by the presence-absence of the world. It also obliterates the boundaries between true and false by repressing all directly lived truth beneath the real presence of the falsehood maintained by the organization of appearances. Individuals who passively accept their subjection to an alien everyday reality are thus driven toward a madness that reacts to this fate by resorting to illusory

magical techniques. The essence of this pseudoresponse to an unanswerable communication is the acceptance and consumption of commodities. The consumer's compulsion to imitate is a truly infantile need, conditioned by all the aspects of his fundamental dispossession. As Gabel puts it in describing a quite different level of pathology, 'the abnormal need for representation compensates for an agonizing feeling of being at the margin of existence.'"[30]

If I had tried to imagine a shape for the space I occupied it would have been circular. I was spinning around the same dilemma that had haunted me for my entire life. How was I going to reach the position of my own image? At 38 I was standing in a warehouse of telemarketers in Beaverton, Oregon and listening to a man ten years my junior lecture me about how I should trust the system. I was watching my young son demand candy and put his sticky hands on the side of this boss's desk. His palm left a mark.

On the way out I decided to stop by my desk and sign the back of my paycheck. I'd check my email while I was there. Maybe my New York editor was willing to redeem me at the last minute? The notes would arrive and I could get back on track—I'd end up as somebody and the small humiliation that was this trip would be erased.

But when I got to my desk something was wrong. The Showtime mug with the smiling serial killer/sociopathic detective was there. The calendar—with photos of a sexy pot dealer dressed only in pot leaves and a call girl with a heart of gold bathing in a martini glass—was tacked the burgundy colored cubicle wall. That was right. But in the space next to mine, in the spot where Walt kept his cup of pens and paper clips, in the area where I'd usually spot his fold out HBO daily aphorisms, there were only empty circle and

---

30) *Debord, Guy, "Society of the Spectacle", Ken Knabb Trans., Bureau of Public Secrets, www.bopsecrets.org, 2002.*

square marks in the dust.

There was nothing on Walt's desk except for these empty spaces and there was a red nylon balloon filled with helium over Walt's chair. In the spot where Walt himself would normally have been there was a balloon with one word printed on it. Instead of "Happy Birthday" or "Get Well Soon" the message printed on the balloon was "Excellent."

I asked Ken, the obese employee on the other side of the cubicle wall, if he'd seen Walt come in, and Ken reported that he had seen Walt. The pod manager had dragged Walt off to a meeting and Walt had yet to return to his desk after that.

"That was three or four hours ago. When you're fired they don't let you collect your stuff after. They tell you and then a security guy escorts you to the parking lot."

Simon climbed onto Walt's chair and smiled. He grabbed the helium balloon in one hand and moved the mouse with the other. He navigated the Comcast desktop with ease, and was on the PBS Kids website before I could object.

"Simon! Get down from there," I said. "What's the deal with the balloon?" I asked.

"Yeah," the kid said. "The girl from Human Resources showed up with that congratulatory balloon right after Walt left for his meeting."

Walt had received the balloon because he'd accomplished what was called a moment of excellence. Somebody in the Quality Department had secretly been listening during one of Walt's sales calls and had determined that the call was good. The balloon was both a reward for good behavior and a reminder that Quality was listening. At the Comcast call center Big Brother was a television program, and the lovely people in Quality were always smiling at you, giving you balloons, and breathing heavily into the phone.

I decided Simon should take the balloon since Walt would never get it, but as we walked across the Comcast call center parking lot, as we approached the light rail station, something inside me clicked or flipped over and I leaned down and looked my son in the eyes.

"How far up do you think that balloon can go?" I asked.

"How far?" Simon asked. He smiled and I could see his tongue sticking out between his teeth, through the gap where a baby tooth had been.

"Do you think it could reach the sun?"

Simon smiled again and then stretched out his left arm and unclenched his left fist. Before he'd really thought about it, he'd let go and the red balloon had gone.

"How far will it go?" he asked. His smile faltered for a moment, but when I took his hand and turned him so he could see it, so he could watch the balloon drift up and up until it was just a speck, until it was invisible, his smile came back.

"What would I have done if I hadn't married your mother and you hadn't been born?" I asked Simon.

He looked confused for a moment and then remembered the question as his own.

"I'd have miss you. I would still have missed you. Even if I didn't know what I was missing or why."

"I can't see it?"

I looked up into the gray sky, scanned the horizon for the red balloon.

"Neither can I."

How to Write Instructions on Situations

"Our era accumulates powers and imagines itself as rational. But no one recognizes these powers as their own. Nowhere is there any entry to adulthood. The only thing that happens is that this long restlessness sometimes eventually evolves into a routinized sleep. Because no one ceases to be kept under guardianship. The point is not to recognize that some people live more or less poorly than others, but that we all live in ways that are out of our control."[31]

In his book *Society of the Spectacle* Debord attacked structuralist thinkers like Lacan for their attempt to transform the separation between the subject and object, between the individual and history, into a universal law. This separation isn't a natural fact, it isn't real, but is the result of living under the sign of the commodity. What must be done is a synthesis of the subject and its object, of the subjective experience of the proletariat and its representation.

But what would such a synthesis look like? That is, how should you represent yourself to yourself? What would this feel like?

When you look to Debord for help along these lines he tells you to live on the margins, to "tend toward a role of pure consumption, particularly the free consumption of your own time …" Turning to Hegel you recall that he solved the mind/body or subject/object split. According to Hegel the very fact that you perceive the split,

---

31) *Debord, Guy, "Critique of Separation", Ken Knabb Trans., Bureau of Public Secrets, www.bopsecrets.org, 2003*

the very recognition of the barrier, indicates that you have already traversed it. If you didn't know what was on the other side then we wouldn't see the barrier to begin with.

In the 1884 science fiction novel *Flatland* by Edwin A. Abbott, two dimensional beings experience the arrival of a cube as a miracle. Never having experienced the third dimension the squares and triangles see the cube as a series of discontinuous appearances. They aren't able to conceive of the idea that the cube has come to them from above because, never having experienced an above, they can't see how the realm above is blocked to them.

Your situation is different. You have experienced history, you have known the world, and you have even already shaped your life directly, but you don't understand how you've done these things.

> "The proletariat will never come to embody power unless it becomes the class of consciousness,"[32]

Instructions on How to Have a Situation

1. Take your ideas, the ones you've written in this book and the others that you may not fully understand, or that you have only just hinted at, into the world with you and apply them.

2. Don't allow yourself to be separated from the community that you want to reject, as this community is your connection to the world. If you hope to bring your ideas into play, this world and its predetermined roles will have to become your tools. New roles can only be added through use of the world as it is.

3. Get some fresh air.

4. Continue to wander.

5. Come home again.

---

32) *Debord, Guy, " Society of the Spectacle", Ken Knabb Trans., Bureau of Public Secrets, 2002*

A Family Dérive

I started the family *dérive* at the Woodstock public library by laying out the tools for the trip underneath the partition shelf where the set of Junior Edition of Britannica Encyclopedias were kept available. I set down my composition notebook, fountain pen, digital camera and three reference books from home on the table next to the computer resource table in the children's library. While Simon played an educational game about a time—traveling car, and Ben chatted on Facebook, I flipped through *The Critique of Everyday Life* by Henri Lefebvre, *The Field Guide of Edible Plants* by Bradford Angier, and *Edward Hopper: Portrait of America* by Wieland Schmied. I opened all three books and compare the messages I found inside.

From Lefebvre's chapter entitled "What is Possible?":

> "When the world the sun shines on is always new, how could everyday life be forever unchangeable, unchangeable in its boredom, its grayness, its repetition of the same actions?"[33]

It was the right question. The question wasn't about justice, capitalist exploitation, self-management, or violence. Lefebvre didn't ask technical questions about production and distribution, or scientific questions about technology and energy. He started with this question:

---

33) *Lefebvre, Henri. "Critique of Everyday Life: Volume 1", John Moore Trans. London, Verso, 1991, pg. 228*

"Why are we bored?"

Page 105 of the Edward Hopper book gave me a kind of answer in the form of a description of Hopper's painting, *People in the Sun*:

> "They are hotel guests who have been tempted out onto the patio to bask in the sun. Wanting to give themselves over to the sun, they have inadvertently put themselves at its mercy. And the sun reveals to all—their inadequacy, the shallowness of their emotional and mental lives [...] Hopper's figures are as vulnerable as Rembrandt's paradise, the paradise of the past, to be forever subjected to harsh light of the present." [34]

When I opened the book on edible plants I found a color photograph of a dandelion.

I sorted through the digital photographs in the camera, trying to weed out the bad shots and make room for more, and stopped on a photo of a duck swimming in a pothole four blocks from our house.

The unpaved roads in our neighborhood are riddled with potholes, but this was the largest pothole I'd ever seen. It was more of a pond than a mere hole. There was a chicken wire fence along the west side of it, and if it hadn't been in the middle of a through street I wouldn't have assumed someone decided his pet duck needed a place to swim.

I told Ben and Simon that we had five more minutes of computer time, and they nodded as if they'd heard me but they didn't stop staring at the screens. Simon's time traveling car was interrogated by a talking tree, while Ben grew corn on Farmville.

I looked down at the camera's screen and flipped through a series of photos of Ben and Simon along another unpaved road. I moved through the sequence fast enough to create a stop motion effect, and watched as Ben and Simon moved into the brush.

---

34) *Schmied, Wieland, Edward Hopper: Portraits of America, New York, Prestel Publishing, 2005*

Simon had insisted that we stop and explore some bushes because he interpreted the arch of branches as a doorway or a portal. He'd been confident that a magical land resided on the other side of the greenery, and while Ben had been less convinced he'd been willing to tag along just to check. I'd hung back to take the photographs.

After another ten minutes I finally dragged the boys away from the computer screens and got them to pick out two books each. My idea for the walk was that we would create a kind of map, or a third mind, first by combining our own books together and second by looking for our own favorite words out in the world. I thought April was the best month for wandering through dandelions in the living alleys, and for mixing literature, ideas, and movement together as we moved outside in the spring rain.

Simon picked out Maurice Sendak's *Where the Wild Things Are* and *Who Needs Donuts* by Mark Alan Stamaky, Ben chose *Harry Potter and Sorcerer's Stone* by J. K. Rowling and *I Am The Cheese* by Robert Cormier, and I chose *The Critique of Everyday Life* by Henri Lefebvre and a book entitled *The Body/Body Problem* by Arthur C. Danto. The words and phrases we chose were: External World, Center Field, Terrible Claws, Alienation, Dinosaur, and Coffee.

"I wanted a donut!" Simon said. "I picked out donut."

I read him the line from his book *Who Needs Donuts* again in an effort to hold firm.

"'It's the coffee that looks like coffee and smells like coffee and tastes like coffee,'" I read. "That's the line you picked."

"But you like coffee and I don't," Simon said.

"Remember, this isn't a scavenger hunt. We might find something that reminds us of coffee, or we might find the word coffee, or we could just use the first letter in the word to direct us. We're not collecting stuff, we're not looking for stuff, we're trying to let whatever is out there move us along."

"Are we going to the coffee shop though?" Ben asked.

"Maybe. It's a wander."

"That's not fair. I don't like coffee," Simon said.

Outside I stopped at Woodstock and 51st and made the boys listen as I read aloud from *The Critique of Everyday Life*. I wanted to explain what we were doing to them again. I wanted to explain it better, but Ben lay down on the curb and closed his eyes when I started reading, apparently adopting a coping strategy of passive resistance. I could not be stopped, but this passivity might succeed where resistance would fail. Even I would eventually grow tired of the sound of my own voice. Simon, on the other hand, wasn't as seasoned and had less self-control. He shouted out interruptions, questions, demands, anything to make me stop.

"This chapter is entitled *What is Possible*. It starts like this: 'When the world the sun shines on is always new, how could everyday life be forever unchangeable in its boredom, its grayness, its repetition of the same actions?'"

"Poop! Diaper!" Simon shouted

"Now you'll just make me start over if you keep up that way."

"Simon, be quiet!" Ben shouted.

"Okay, here goes: 'When the world the sun—'"

"Do wizards live in Portland?" Simon asked to interrupt.

"What?"

"Poop!"

"Okay, look I just want to read aloud all the way to the bottom of the page. 'To study philosophy as an indirect criticism of life is to perceive everyday life—"

"Stop! Stop! Stop!"

The first item on our list of words were 'terrible claws', and we set off up Woodstock, away from the library and toward 52nd, with lobsters and/or werewolves on our minds. We would find claws and see where they pointed, but Simon started complaining again.

"I don't want to get coffee," he said.

"We won't get coffee," I said. "If we go to a coffee place you can have chocolate milk."

"No. I don't want to go to a coffee shop."

"I said if. If we go."

But, Simon saw through me. The idea had gained a hold on me. I wanted an espresso drink and had already decided to be sure to stop by Papaccinos on 46th before going back home. I'd put it off for a while, get through the list, or all the other words, before going for coffee.

"It's not fair," Simon said.

"Look, we're not on the word coffee. The first word is claws. Terrible claws."

We stopped on the corner of 52nd and Woodstock, and I looked across at the empty building that once had been an Arby's restaurant but which was now just an ugly empty shell. The Arby's Corporation builds each restaurant in its franchise the same, and any differences you might find when comparing one restaurant to another just indicates the era within which each building was constructed. The abandoned building on the corner of 52nd and Woodstock looked to have been built in the late 80s or early 90s— the pseudo tin roof made of plastic panels and the red concrete stripe along the side were both references to modernist tropes, too self-aware to have been designed before Reagan.

"It's too bad Arby's closed," Ben said.

"You hungry?"

"A little bit." Ben was thirteen and almost always hungry.

"We could get something to eat," I said.

"Where?"

"Don't ask where," I said.

"I don't want to go to the coffee shop," Simon said. "I want a donut!"

I waved at Simon, trying not to respond in a big way and to just use a comic gesture instead. But Simon wasn't having any of it.

"Is that a claw?" Ben asked.

"Where?"

Ben pointed to an orange mitten in a puddle of oil along the curb. He pointed to a small orange wool mitten stranded and dipped in the street, and I yelped when Simon stepped off the curb and knelt down to look closer. I stepped forward and grabbed his hand, jerked him back to me.

"It's not a claw," he said.

"You can't go into the street like that."

"It's a glove," he said. And he held it up to me. He held up the dirty orange glove. It seemed like a terrible claw to me.

The words we were looking for, again, were External World, Center Field, Alienation, Dinosaur, and Coffee.

We found dinosaur prints everywhere and it was Simon who was the first to notice them. Every puddle, every large indentation in the unpaved roads, had to have been left there by some creature or another, Simon reasoned, and given the size of these puddles, potholes, and duck ponds it only made sense that Dinosaurs were the culprits. He stopped at the edge of one of the mid—sized puddles, looked at his own reflection in the dirty water, and then took a few steps back and tried for a running leap across.

"Your Keds are soaked," I said.

"It's all right."

"We should go home."

"It's okay," Simon said.

We found Center Field in Woodstock park right behind Woodstock Elementary. We walked the white lines around to each base, and then stood together on the grass beyond this. Woodstock Park is populated by deciduous trees, dogs off their leashes, school children, and some red brick boxes constructed by the artist Lloyd Hamrol. Each of us took a turn standing on the nearest brick sculpture and looking down at the others.

We looked for the word Alienation in the Bi-Mart on Woodstock and 43rd. I enjoyed Bi-Mart nostalgically as the store's interior, its red and white signs and numbered aisles, was unselfconsciously retro, while Ben seemed to enjoy the subversive nature looking for the word alienation in this corporate environment. He liked standing apart from the objects and people around him and analyzing what made a packet of gummy worms or an aisle full of office supplies corrupted.

"The problem here is that the entire store could be thought of as alienating. Each commodity is bit of alienated labor," I said.

"Can I get a toy?" Simon asked.

"No!" Ben said.

"I don't think so."

"Ah, come on. One toy?"

"No promises."

Simon took off running toward the toy aisle.

We examined Fisher Price machine guns, Toxic Slime made by Mattel, and polymorphously perverse Elmo and I tried to explain Marx's labor theory of value. Ben listened carefully as we flipped through a rack of Justin Bieber posters, and Simon pulled items off the shelf, approaching me with possible purchases.

"What about this?" he asked. He'd picked out a white plastic figurine called a Color Blank, a toy that masqueraded as an art project. The particular Color Blank was named Blockhead, its head a blank cube that welcomed you were to draw on. He came with three permanent markers: black, red, and yellow.

I checked the word Alienation from my list and then considered the last item: "External World."

"Okay," I said. "Now we can get coffee."

"I don't want to get coffee."

"I'll get coffee and you can have that Color Blank and a hot chocolate."

"I can have this?" Simon asked and held up the little man with the blank face.

"Yes."

How were we ever to find our way to the External World? Alienation, Center Field, and Dinosaurs were easy, but this was hard. The World was either everywhere all around us, or it was nowhere at all. To find it, to know we'd found it, this would be the same kind of miracle as creating a situation out of everyday life.

Section Three: Foraging for Change (the present)

The Limbo of a Firing

In Kafka's novel *The Trial* the bureaucracy appears as a decrepit ruin; falling apart, dusty, stale, the bowels of the system are full of holes, and yet the system itself is somehow stronger for it. The weakness of the structure is perversely its strength. In Orson Welles' film version of the Kafka's novel, Anthony Perkins is called to attend a preliminary hearing for his trial while he is attending the theater. There is no official telegram, and no formal sounding officer reaches him by phone, but rather an innocuous note is passed to him by a fellow theatergoer. The woman who passes him the note knows nothing about the business she's participating in. It is in this way, during an otherwise normal and untroubled daily discourse, that authority, in both the novel and the film, is made objective. Power floats weightless and is always out of the line of sight.

When my supervisor at Comcast informed me that I might be fired from my cubicle job at the Beaverton call center, he did not make a big production out of getting my attention, but simply tapped me on the shoulder while I was at work selling what we called CHSI (Comcast's High Speed Internet). When I turned to see who was tapping, I found my twenty-something supervisor, who always appeared to me to have walked off the set of an HBO original series. He was already talking to another salesman over the cubicle wall. He was smiling and laughing, apparently distracted from his

106

task in the time it took me to turn around.

"Got a second?" he asked when he turned back to me.

This is how I discovered that I was under the threat of possible termination for my failure to offer a customer the opportunity of adding a land line phone to their cable and internet service. In fact, he didn't tell me I was fired right away, but rather I was pulled aside, taken off the phones, and taken to the dim back room office of the human resource director. If my immediate supervisor looked like Vincent Chase from *Entourage*, the human resources director looked something more like Mr. Clean. Bald and Corporate and perhaps just a touch queer.

"Can you tell us why you didn't offer this customer phone service?" he wanted to know. And I started to relax. If they were going to fire me for this infraction I could at least be secure in the knowledge that the punishment didn't fit the crime. The rule and its implementation were absurd, but too blatantly so, and if Kafka had been writing the scene he'd have aimed to spread the absurdity around. The point is always to involve the accused in the passing of judgment. For example, in *The Trial* the police do not charge the protagonist with anything, but by treating him as guilty they inspire his guilt. In my case, by telling me so directly what it was that I'd done, Mr. Clean and my Vincent had let me off the hook.

Furthermore, sometimes a theory can be a useful thing. When you are working in a suburban call center for a major telecommunications corporation and find that you are subject to absurd rules—rules that are not only cumbersome and inhibiting but that even contradict one another. So, in order to function at all, one must break them. When precariousness is the inevitable result of the way a job is structured, it helps to know why management is always pushed to push the workers in this way. It's helpful to seek some sort of big picture when faced with personal woes.

As the YouTube star Brendan Cooney wrote in his description for his YouTube video, Law of Value 6: Socially Necessary Labor Time:

> "Our private labor doesn't immediately become social. It must become value in order to be social. But in becoming value it is disciplined by socially necessary labor time. SNLT acts as an external force which disciplines our private labor, constantly compelling us to work more efficiently, yet never actually making our work easier or more fulfilling."[35]

It's probably worth noting that before Cooney a writer named Marx made a similar point. And while it's easy enough to get lost in the history of debate around Marx's labor theory of value and various definitions of Socially Necessary Labor Time, this much is fairly certain. After the economic downturn of 2008 many, many more customer were calling in to downgrade or shut off their cable services. In order to make up this loss in revenue the sales department was being disciplined in the hopes that such discipline would make us more efficient. Before the downturn we could be confident that as long as we were making sales we would be secure in our jobs, but now we were being asked to be more efficient on every call. We had to push the product harder.

This was why my job was in jeopardy, and the fact that I had sold two of the three products possible during the call, that the customer had required an instant installation and this foreclosed the possibility of adding the third product, none of this mattered. What mattered was discipline on the floor, and if that put some employees in a double bind (one could just as easily be fired for failing to meet quota while adhering to the new efficiency protocol as for failing to adhere), why this didn't matter either. The given high employment churn and downsizing was another efficiency.

I understood all of this. They could fire me, but they couldn't

---

35) Cooney, Brendan. "Law of Value 6: Socially Necessary Labor Time," distributed by YouTube, 2011

touch me, or so I thought.

Their final trick was not firing me outright, but they were going to think it over first. They were going to keep me on the phones, let me dangle, let me think over the full implication of the term misconduct, and then (when the newly hired sales team was ready to hit the floor) they'd fire me.

Going back to my desk, the question that whirled around my head wasn't whether or not the rule itself is just, but whether the rule was just a cover story. Given the absurdity of the rule it can't have been applied for the reasons that were explicitly stated. This meant that perhaps there were other, more reasonable, charges standing behind the absurd charges. Somehow guilt found me, and once the feeling came to me I looked for a reason for it. The feeling had to attach to something.

What had I done to give power an excuse to exercise its arbitrary will? Had I been too rude or too lazy? Had I been less than adequately friendly, or insufficiently social?

As I returned to my desk, two competing questions spun around in my head. The first one was, what was wrong with me that I'd been fired from such a low level job? And the second question was, why do we all put up with it? How did the spectacle of Comcast reproduce itself daily, and what was the connection between the content the company provided (MTV, HBO or The Playboy Channel, etc ...) and the compensatory activities and beliefs that ensured that we stayed in our cubicles?

And it turned out that the answers to these two questions were identical to each other.

The heroes of hipster Hollywood impose the corporations' cynical hedonism through the critical distance implied in every line of dialog in such programs as *Californication* or *Entourage*. Both shows undermine and support the corporate culture. And the logic that reproduces daily life at Comcast is a strange loop or a knot.

For example, one must always be out for one's self on the job and one must be willing to cheat and to lie in order to get ahead on the job. This is what we were secretly taught in our training class, and were more overtly taught during the daily practice of selling cable. However, one must never be caught cheating and lying to the customer. In order to get ahead in the system one must finally stop recognizing cheating and lying as cheating and lying and view instead as using the right language. If one internalizes the lying deeply enough then one can never be caught.

Or as the anti-psychiatrist R. D. Laing stated in his 1969 poetry book/psychiatric rant, *Knots*:

They are playing a game.

They are playing at not

Playing a game.

If I show them I see they are,

I Shall break the rules and they will punish me

I must play their game, of not seeing I see the game.

And here's another approach to saying the same thing: If a cubicle had four walls instead of three, the worker would realize that he was trapped, but with just three walls the worker is free to stay in his cubicle.

James Bond: Urban Forager

When a worker in any field is alerted to the fact that unemployment is immanent there are various recommended responses. The first and most commonly given piece of advice is simply to remain calm. This serves everyone well. You are less likely to burn bridges, break office equipment, or serve time in jail if you follow this injunction from *The Hitchhiker's Guide to the Galaxy*:

"Don't panic."

But, after you've counted to thirty and taken a deep breath, what is the best way to deal the news of your sudden redundancy? The experts are conflicted. Some suggest that you quietly rewrite your resume, others tell you to announce your termination to the world and make sure that everyone who might be of some use to you in your new job search is alerted to your need. Still others suggest that you contact a lawyer, especially if you suspect that your employer may try to block your efforts to collect unemployment. (And if there is one piece of advice in this book that is worth taking, it is probably not found in the preceding line.) Still, the most obvious course of action after receiving such news is almost never overtly recommended:

Get a drink.

In my case I met with an old friend at the Horse Brass Pub in Southeast Portland. The Horse Brass is an authentic British pub with plaster walls made yellow by decades of cigarette smoke inside, and with dartboards, dark wood booths, and neon signs for micro—brewed and imported beers and lagers. The place serves hundreds of different brews and I aimed to try them all, or at least enough to almost, but not quite, put myself off beer and lager for the rest of my life.

My friend and interlocutor for this devolution into incoherence turned out to be an ersatz amalgamation of my long-term friend, James Farris, and Glenn Bond, my mailman. James had started out as a colleague in the 90s when I was just twenty. I'd worked several jobs for arts and political organizations with him over the years. Besides delivering my mail, Glenn Bond most frequently challenged me to a game of chess over several lagers. While I'd never worked with Glenn, my family was mixed up with his. His wife and my wife were close, as were his children to mine.

And this is how I ended up consulting with James Bond.

> "In these conditions [when] a financier can be a singer, a lawyer a police spy, a baker can parade his literary tastes, an actor can be president... it happens that the mediatic transition provides the cover for many enterprises, officially independent but in fact secretly linked by various ad hoc networks. For example, one can now publish a novel in order to arrange an assassination. Such picturesque examples also go to show that one should never trust someone because of their job. But the greatest ambition of the integrated spectacular is still that secret agents become revolutionaries, and that revolutionaries become secret agents."[36]

"What is the plan, Mister Lain?" James Bond asked me. Imagine, if you will, that Michael Caine was performing the role.

My plan was simple—go feudal. That is, if the factories were all shutting down and the welfare state had been relegated to the

---

36) Debord, Guy, *"Comments on the Society of the Spectacle"*, Bill Brown Trans., Not Bored Website, http://www.notbored.org/commentaires.html

dustbin of history, perhaps returning to the land, whatever tiny piece of it that I might be able to get my hands on, would be my last and best option. Besides, even if there were more high-tech drone positions available in some cubicle farm somewhere, I didn't want any part of that any more.

Subsistence farming, or hunting and gathering, those were my big ideas.

The waitress brought me a plate of bangers and mash and I pondered what it would entail to produce my own bangers. I decided that such delicacies would be less available in my future. Squash, on the other hand, would be plentiful.

James Bond told me that his job gathering surveys for movie studios at the Lloyd Center Mall and his job delivering the mail in suburbia, was slowly killing him. He'd worked about 9 days straight, 10 hour days on his feet. He was sick of the smell of Orange Juliuses, sick of asking obese mall walkers for their thoughts about Dwayne Johnson in *The Tooth Fairy* and/or John Cusack in *2012*. He was sick of delivering junk mail, bills, Netflix envelopes and nothing else.

"Who would have predicted that in the year 2010, kitchen gardens and foraging were going to look to be sensible solutions to the problems of day to day life? When I defeated Hugo Drax on *Moonraker* I thought the space age was just beginning. I anticipated we'd all have personal helicopters," Bond said.

"Did you?"

He shrugged and looked at the pub's list of brews. "I wonder if they serve a decent martini."

"Maybe this new future we're heading for will be like a reality show. Wasn't there one like what you're describing? With Paris Hilton on an Amish farm?"

The more I drank the better the idea seemed to me, and when I started seeing double, it was settled. Every criticism or problem Mr. Bond could come up with or discover just confirmed the idea.

"People can't grow their own food individually, not all of it," he said.

"Perfect. That will mean we'll be forced to work collectively."

"Even collectively, using everyone's backyards, it probably wouldn't be enough."

"That will force us to acquire collective land."

"Okay, but what about water. What about seed? How are you going to acquire the seed?"

And that's when I realized that this James Bond, this strange combination of Charles Bukowski and Jonathan Winters, might not be trustworthy. He raised his martini glass to me as it all came together. I really would have to revolt. Even if I wanted to be a simple hippie peasant, I'd have to seize the means of production. There was no other way out.

Plums, Ben, and Family

The tree in our neighbor's front yard was weighed down by thousands of golf ball-sized plums, so many that hundreds had dropped off before ripening. Sour purple balls of fruit littered the sidewalk and gutter on 51st. This blue house with purple trim and overburdened plum tree became the first target for our foraging effort after everything else seemed to fall to pieces.

When we went to ring the bell we found two signs above the mail slot. The first sign read simply, no soliciting. The other, the sign even higher up, at eye level, read "Beware of the Witch" and was decorated with a rainbow-colored pentagram. We rang the bell, hoping that the witch would be an ally, that she would be sympathetic to our cause.

The woman who opened the door was dressed all in denim. She was forty or so years old, and while she had a tattoo of a pentagram on her neck and a pierced lip, the whole ensemble she was wearing gave her away. She wasn't tough or scary, but simply liked to play dress-up. Her motorcycle witch persona was just another version of Pacific Northwest bohemia.

There was no problem. She would be glad if we took as many tiny plums as we could carry. She was sick of plums and could eat no more of them. Her entire household had had its fill of plums.

"Go to it," she said.

After returning home for a step ladder and a few canvas bags, my son and I set to work picking. Some of the plums were hard and sour, many were overripe and would squish in our hands, leaving our fingers sticky. But many were just right and after 15 or 20 minutes, we'd both developed an eye for the plum. We searched out dark purple skin and firm, round flesh.

We made a game out of it, a competition. We filled several canvas bags with plums, took turns on the ladder, but always Ben would urge me to hurry up and give him a chance, or I would sigh impatiently when our roles were reversed.

"Which of us has more?" Ben asked.

It seemed natural that picking plums should become a competition. Anything could become a contest, a way to prove oneself. If two Lain men were involved, almost any event could become a competition.

I recalled visiting my grandfather in Norris, Tennessee in the early 80s and setting out into his backyard forest in search of mushrooms. Grandpa had proven himself by picking mushrooms from the mossy forest floor and confidently taking a bite of the fungus's gray flesh. My father had proven himself by walking fast and breaking away from the rest of us. Like a scout in a battle, he'd take off up the path and then circle back and report on what was coming. And my job, my way of winning, had been to remain focused in the moment and keep up. I had a tendency to get lost in my thoughts and dawdle behind.

"Which of us have picked more plums? Who is faster?" Benjamin asked.

I told him that I wasn't keeping track, but I held out my canvas sack so he could make his own assessment. I had about twice as many plums as him, and to catch up, he started to hunt down still-intact plums that had fallen in the grass around the tree.

This was what it meant to be a father. It was unseemly to be seen as competing, yet one had a duty to win. A teen son, especially, needed his father to win.

In R. D. Laing's 1969 book, *The Politics of the Family,* he states that, "between truth and lie are images we imagine and think are real, that paralyze our imagination and our thinking in our efforts to conserve them."

I remember hiking near Norris Dam Park with my grandfather and father in 1978 or 1979. We came up on the Gristmill and after admiring the landmark, after discussing what the water wheel and gears inside were used for (I can't recall now if grain was crushed in the mill, or if something more esoteric occurred behind the old dark wood), another contest started up. The trick was to see how fast we could run, and how quickly the wheel would turn.

All three of us took a position inside the wheel and like hamsters or mice we began to run. The wheel turned and increased in speed. The spinning wheel moved faster and faster, until I was running so fast that I felt I was going to stumble. I couldn't keep up and so I stopped and was carried away. My father and grandfather were suddenly ahead and then underneath me as I moved with the wheel.

I don't remember if they stopped before I reached the top, or if I reached the top, or if I somehow made it all the way around. But I'd like to think I came back on them from the other side. I do recall that the spinning seemed like some sort of magic trick. We'd started a mechanism, wound a spring with a simple movement and just by stopping it was possible to fly.

"How many plums do you have now?" Ben wanted to know.

I showed him the contents of my bag again.

Picking miniature plums in our neighbor's yard, I imagined that she might be watching us from her kitchen window. I imagined her kitchen was painted yellow and white, that it was colored to appear as if it was always full of sunlight. Her kitchen was clean. I wondered if she might come back out to talk to us. Would she bring a book about local plants with glossy photographs of flowering bushes and stalks of green leaves? Would she bring us ginger lemonade or some of her hippie drink? Or would she just stay inside in the yellow, and watch us.

It was no surprise that picking plums should become a competition between father and son. What else could such an endeavor be for us? What other kind of game was there to play?

In the essay *Lacan: At What Point is He Hegelian?* Slavoj Zizek claims that nature (and women) do not exist. He says that it is impossible to return to some pre-Oedipal world, to find some innocent game to play, not because the Oedipus game is ordained by God, not because the original father turned a dirty trick, but rather because the very idea of an original innocence, something out beyond the game we're playing, is a key concept in this Oedipus game itself. Using nature as an escape route from technological capitalism is like putting hotels on Boardwalk and Park Place as an escape route from a game of Monopoly.

"In this precise sense Woman is one of the names of the father."[37]

I wondered if we appeared to be a happy family to her, or if we might seem too happy, maybe dully adjusted, and thereby just a couple of fools. And I worked harder at collecting the plums faster. I worked harder to stay ahead of my 13-year-old, and worked hard to keep him from seeing me work hard.

Remember that the woman watching us was a witch. She was the one who I was secretly entertaining, the one I wanted to impress with my bag of seeded fruit. My son, on the other hand, probably

---

37) Zizek, Slavoj, *"Lacan: At What Point is He Hegelian" Rex Butler Trans., www. lacan.com/zizlacan1.html*

only wanted to impress me by beating me at his game.

But in any case, what does it mean to be a witch or a sorcerer? According to the New Age writer and anthropologist Carlos Castaneda a Yaqui sorcerer is the one who realizes that the world of everyday life is only a description. The sorcerer understandings that the world outside the self is a fiction, and is the one who can thereby alter the outer world by altering the description.

> "Do you know that you can extend yourself forever in any directions I have pointed to?" Don Juan asked. "If you had enough power my words alone would serve as the means for you to round up the totality of yourself and to get the crucial part of it out of the boundaries in which it is contained."[38]

This is the sorcerer, the man who can through his personal power be himself totally, but in order for such a sorcerer to exist he must imagine another. And who is this? The other is the phallic mother. She is reality without description, what is really real out there beyond description, and yet she has not been cut. She is empty, without words or perceptible qualities, and yet she is full and complete.

What is a witch? She is a paradox. She is a contradiction. Most of all, she is a child's dream.

Tales of Power by Carlos Castaneda starts out with the author's appointment with a moth. The story is supported by the secret supposition that there is a way to knowledge. That there is a story being acted out. That is the guru/student relationship. The guru is the one who is desired by the big other and who can thereby tell the student the story.

The Guru is taking the place of the Big Other—it isn't as though a story wasn't already acting itself out, but rather this story is challenged by the little other of the guru. The secret knowledge

---

38) Castaneda, Carlos. *Tales of Power*, Simon and Schuster Inc., New York, 1974.

appears to be the fictional status of the original story, however there are two difficulties:

1. Distinguishing when one has abandoned the first story's impossible to do on one's own. Thus the guru tells him.

2. The achievement of telling one's own story is impossible.

But why is it impossible?

The belief in a Kantian split between the internal subjective self and the real nominative self is the cause behind Castaneda's misunderstanding. The story, the description, which is the objective world is taken to be real while Castaneda's subjective perceptions are not real. The solution to this internal split, as put forward by Hegel, is to understand that the very recognition of the gap between the subjective sense of self and the perceptual phenomena that represent the world itself implies that the gap has been traversed. This doesn't mean that there is no gap, but rather that there is no big Other. The gap itself is real.

We ended up with more plums than we could eat before the excess went bad. They were small round and sweet. We could have frozen them, but my wife decided to make the plums into a fruit butter.

She boiled away the skins, stirred in sugar, and set the mixture in the fridge to cool. Since this was her first attempt, the plums congealed into a firm, sticky mass. The rubbery result tasted good, like a fruit candy, but it was nothing like butter. You could never spread this concoction on toast.

The unworkable mass of these foraged plums is precisely how the other, the witch, the father's excessive underside, or the woman is real. As sweet and as compelling as it was, my son and I could not resist cutting slices of the sticky mass and sucking fragments down. The plums had been transformed into something that really could not fit, and in this way we held ourselves at a distance from the dish. We hovered around the purple mess, but couldn't bring ourselves to consume it in any proper way. Unadulterated food, free food, natural food was in front of us, accessible in its bowl, but even as we partook we were separated from it. This was the surplus, the excess of our current system and as such, it reinforced the current system.

Of course, once one sees how our foraged plums reinforced the current food economy (by representing a nature that is always separated off from human life) then the plums cease to be natural at all. They expose themselves as another sticky mess.

Comcast as Super-Ego

"Initiating Comcast Xfinity upgrade in 3 ... 2 ... 1 ..."
—from 2010 Comcast Advertisement

According to the psychoanalyst Lacan, the super-ego relies upon the inevitably of the ego's failure to adequately fulfill the super-ego's requirements for its continued power. For example, in Kafka's story "The Judgment," George's continual guilty efforts to do right by everyone, to fulfill his duty as a friend and a son, ultimately emboldens K.'s infirm father to leap from his bed and pass sentence (death by drowning).

> "Up to this point you've known only about yourself! Essentially you've been an innocent child, but even more essentially you've been a devilish human being! And therefore understand this: I sentence you now to death by drowning!"[39]

And when, as an obedient son, K. goes to the nearest bridge and plunges himself beneath the waves, even this self-termination is ultimately a failure because, after all, the flip side of his father's injunction to suicide was the challenge to his son; find a way to live.

"Initiating Comcast Xfinity upgrade in 3 ... 2 ... 1 ..."

During my final week as an employee at Comcast I witnessed how the corporate capitalist super-ego functions today. I witnessed not only how any given corporate injunction always contains a reversal, but also how the dissolution of the appearance of the super-ego (or

---

39) Kafka, Franz, "The Judgment," Ian Johnston Trans., Franz Kafka Online, http://www.kafka-online.info/-the-judgement.html)

the way the corporation commands his children to freedom and self-actualization), leads to cognitive dissonance, boundary dissolution, and a psychotic break.

> "Traditionally, psychoanalysis has been expected to enable the patient to overcome the obstacles preventing his or her access to normal sexual satisfaction... but now we are bombarded from all sides by the injunction to 'Enjoy!'. Maybe psychoanalysis should perhaps be regarded differently? Psychoanalysis is the only discourse in which you are allowed not to enjoy ..."[40]

In the new corporate culture nothing is a big deal. Everything is small and real because the era of hierarchies and totalizing institutionalized discourses is over. And the rules, if they can be said to exist at all, are constantly in flux. If you don't keep up with your emails, if you don't read that tweet, if you don't crush it using everything you've got as a unique individual, then you'll miss the cluetrain.

> "Mediocrity is for losers! If given the choice of five places to eat lunch, are you going to pick the mediocre one? Given the choice of five people to hire, are you going to pick the mediocre one? ...Who picks the average, who picks the mediocre? Nobody!"[41]

The Corporation as super-ego condemns us not to death by drowning, but to a life lived as completely as possible. We are asked for nothing other than total mastery and creativity because, after all, in the new normal one has to be a master of the universe just to survive.

In my last few days at Comcast, during the twilight days of my time inside the machine, I saw the thing itself. The gap between signifier and signified.

---

40) *Zizek, Slavoj, "Freud Lives!" London Review of books, Vol. 28, No. 10, May 2006, http://www.lrb.co.uk/v28/n10/slavoj-zizek/freud-lives*
41) *Godin, Seth, "TED Talk: A Purple Cow," distributed by Vimeo, http://vimeo. com/384049*

My Dinner With Andre

"You see, I think it's quite possible that the nineteen-sixties represented the last burst of the human being before he was extinguished. And that this is the beginning of the rest of the future now, and that from now on there'll simply be all these robots walking around, feeling nothing, thinking nothing."

—Andre in the film *My Dinner With Andre*

The other day I was listening to *My Dinner with Andre* on YouTube while writing SEO sentences. While watching, I remembered that my best friend from high school, Miriam's old boyfriend, considered this film middle class pseudo-intellectual drivel. This high school friend is now a literature/film professor in Edmonton.

Living in the age of the internet meant that I could simply call up Facebook and ping him about it. I sent him the following message:

"I just watched *My Dinner with Andre* on YouTube and thought of you. Do you still think the ideas in *My Dinner with Andre* are just a collection of New York/New Age twaddle?"

And while I was on Facebook I asked my virtual friends what they thought of the film and immediately received this response from a science fiction writer living in Arizona:

"It's on the tiny list of movies that Emma and I walked out of. We thought we knew too many people like the main characters. But maybe it was just the wrong night, 'cause a lot of people we respect think it's a great movie. Maybe the answer is it's both middle class twaddle and brilliant."

What was it about the characters that this science fiction writer and my old friend both recognized and despised? Which character was the one they disliked? Rewatching the movie on my computer, listening to it rather than watching, I certainly felt the characters were familiar, but I didn't find Wally and Andre particularly off-putting. Recognizing these two as types didn't alter or mitigate the main point of the film. *My Dinner with Andre* was a film grappling with its moment in history, with the failures of the previous two decades. Yes, it's staged in New York. Yes, the two characters are limousine liberals. But New York was still the center of Western culture, and who else but two limousine liberals could make their worrying about the historical moment into a Hollywood film?

Consider this quote:

ANDRE: We're bored. We're all bored now. But has it ever occurred to you, Wally, that the process that creates this boredom that we see in the world now, may very well be a self perpetuating, unconscious form of brainwashing created by a world totalitarian government based on money and that all of this is much more dangerous than one thinks, and its not just a question of individual survival, Wally, but that somebody who's bored is asleep, and somebody who's asleep will not say no?

Now there are definitely things to pick apart in this quote, and throughout the picture Andre's mysticism and new age adventures all stand in the way of his understanding. He's constantly mystifying what is in fact a social dilemma. But, while he describes all these New Age conferences and meditations and magic rituals he's been involved with, in the end he comes to the conclusion that he's been acting like a little prince. There is a self-awareness at work in the character and in the movie itself.

So the question remains. Is my enjoyment of this movie a symptom of my middle class consciousness, is the rejection of the movie a symptom, or am I asking the wrong question?

Perhaps *My Dinner with Andre* wasn't really a movie at all, or maybe it's no longer a movie now.

A few hours later I received word back from my old high school buddy, the professor in Canada.

"Man, I've tried to type this response like three times, and Facebook keeps logging me out. Anyway, if memory serves, I first saw this in high school and thought it was great, then I saw it right after university, and hated it. I just realized that a few years ago I wrote a piece for the local weekly on a Louis Malle retrospective, and I didn't even mention *My Dinner With Andre*. So I guess I've moved through admiration, past contempt and into indifference."

"Can you really watch the entire thing on YouTube?"

I wrote:

"Yes. The whole thing is on YouTube. All you have to do is click on the link and watch it ten minutes at a time."

My Dinner with Andre offers up two different reactions to the failure of the sixties, to the failure of the New Left. There is Wallace Shawn's humble but obviously narcissistic retreat, and there is Andre's similarly narcissistic but utterly manic search for the real. Andre searches for reality and instead falls into the imaginary. Neither character can bring themselves to see their problems as social problems that stem from the way their society goes about producing and distributing power in the world. But they verge on arriving at such a view.

ANDRE: Because somehow in our social existence today we're only allowed to express our feelings weirdly and indirectly. If you express them directly everybody goes crazy!

The unreality of 1981, the crazed spectacle that was self-evident then today threatens to overwhelm us. And all around these two solutions—a retreat into humble consumption and acceptance, or a retreat into the imaginary and a grasping after the real—are returning with a vengeance.

I wrote back to my old friend: "Can you remember what you hated about it? Was it because you didn't see it as a good use of cinema that inspired you're contempt? Because I'm not really interested in it as a film. I'm interested in the ideas, in the conversation."

WALLY: Yeah, but I mean, I would never give up my electric blanket, Andre. I mean, because New York is cold in the winter. I mean, our apartment is cold! It's a difficult environment. I mean, our life is tough enough as it is. I'm not looking for ways to get rid of a few things that provide relief and comfort. I mean, on the contrary, I'm looking for more comfort because the world is very abrasive. I mean, I'm trying to protect myself because, really, there's these abrasive beatings to be avoided everywhere you look!

ANDRE: But, Wally, don't you see that comfort can be dangerous? I mean, you like to be comfortable and I like to be comfortable too, but comfort can lull you into a dangerous tranquility?

It's a fairly simple observation, but consider how so many on the Marxist left came to the conclusion that the consumer utopia of the 50s and 60s had undone their revolutionary project. Ponder Slavoj Zizek's joke that the US has a working class, but it's in China. The challenge to rejecting comfort is serious. Can only little princes like Andre find the solid ground from which they can reject the comfort of the electric blanket?

This isn't a movie. It's a document of a conversation that was important then and even more vital now.

It isn't a movie, it never was a movie. Thirty years later it is time that we transcended that perception of it. It has always been a real conversation between two New York big shots put on the big screen as a movie, and today *My Dinner with Andre* is just one more part of the culture that we need to seize, to occupy.

Getting Fired

Kafka is reported to have laughed while reading aloud passages from his book *The Trial* to his friends at the Cafe Arco. His descriptions of a K. wracked with guilt, a K. who, even during his execution, wondered if he might've forgotten something or failed to try hard enough, struck Kafka as funny. It's reported that Kafka had to stop and gasp for air as he read along.

> "As his eyes grew dim, K. could still make out the two men near his face, their cheeks touching as they observed the crucial moment. It was as if the shame of it should outlive him."[42]

But it is not just K. who is absurd. The executioners are also bizarre and even obscene in how they handle themselves, and in how they act out their subjective innocence. They plunged a knife into a K.'s heart and twisted it, but didn't have the decency to howl with pleasure. Instead they stared blankly at him, and in this way, they shirked responsibility. In fact, this dumb stare was precisely a further condemnation of K., and as such it was a secondary violence. Their faces remained blank because the victim was so far beneath them, that he didn't even excite their rage or enjoyment.

On the day that I was fired I refused to stay at my desk. My supervisor had me continue to work as if nothing was going to change. I was asked to watch a training video announcing the implementation of Xfinity, a propaganda piece that aimed to

---

42) *Kafka, Franz, "The Trial" David Wyllie Trans., Project Gutenberg, 2003*

convince the employees and public that this change of name was something more than a legalistic trick employed so that Comcast could buy NBC without violating anti-trust laws, but I refused to play along. I left the propaganda running on my computer while I roamed between the cubicle walls to find somebody in authority.

The reason I'd been given for my termination was absurd and if I could find someone in authority with a bit of sense I'd be able to explain everything and keep my shit job. I hated them all by this point. All the managers, all the Comcastic employees were killing me, but my understanding that the job was killing me did nothing to slow my pursuit of a means by which to hang onto it.

> "Was help still possible? Were there objections that had not been voiced? Surely there were ..."[43]

I finally found Roger, the supervisor for the call center, in his office. But Roger told me that he'd already been made aware of the circumstances and that the HR guy, Mister Clean, would be contacting me by the end of the day. I asked Roger if he was aware of the absurd quality of the situation, if he saw the double-bind I was in, and Roger looked at me blankly. All I was going to be able to get from him were directions on how to find the door.

The best way I can describe my final encounter with Mister Clean and my hipster supervisor is to reference an animated sequence from the BBC comedy sketch program Monty Python's Flying Circus.

I recall that a cardboard cutout of a lemur or a snow monkey turned a crank so that gears moved inside the Kodachrome body of a mincing Charles Atlas. Atlas shrugged and then swallowed the furniture inside his luxurious and appealing living room. Finally, cherubs flew into the picture, leaving divine droppings on the orange carpet. They grabbed Charles Atlas by his shoulders in

---

43) *Kafka, Franz, "The Trial" David Wyllie Trans., Project Gutenberg, 2003*

order to to deliver him to the open maw of Leonardo's Mona Lisa. She swallowed him whole.

Mister Clean wanted me to sign a statement that justified my termination in terms of misconduct. I refused. I asked what consequence might be imposed on me if I declined to sign. And when Mister Clean seemed stumped I met him halfway and said that I'd sign if they eliminated the word misconduct. After all, Oregon is an at-will state and there was no denying that they were terminating me.

"Just write down that I'm terminated without cause and I'll sign."

"We won't be changing the language of this document."

"Then I won't be signing it. What happens now?"

My supervisor wrote a note where I'd been meant to sign and then initialed the note.

The note read: "Employee refused to sign."

How to Write Instruction on Foraging

You find writing a set of instructions on foraging is an impossible task for three reasons. Firstly, the plant life in any given reader's neighborhood will vary (the ground cherry's habitat includes recently cultivated fields, while soap weed grows alongside roadsides and in dry pastures), secondly, the plants are difficult to describe with words (the hobblebrush produces red fruit in round-topped clusters, the highbrush cranberry produces red berries in round-topped clusters), and thirdly, the true object of foraging is not the fruits and berries one might find, but nature itself. Writing directly about foraging is so difficult because when you attempt to write about nature you either end up cataloging animals and plants or writing about ideas, and everyone knows that there is nothing natural about idea. An idea is the opposite of what is natural.

As the psychotic science fiction writer Philip K. Dick wrote back in the 70s, "Nature is real. And Reality is whatever sticks around even if you ignore it."

Your ideas, on the other hand, are fleeting. They stick around only for as long as you pay attention. The trick is distinguishing what has truly stuck around even when you've stopped thinking about it, that real stuff out there, from those ideas that return as a habit of thought. Or, put another way, in material terms, the trouble is between distinguishing what plants or other features of the landscape would exist if nobody was around to disturb anything.

In Thomas S. Elias and Peter Dykeman's book *Edible Wild Plants*, the authors make it clear that such a real world doesn't exist. Instead, wild plants always emerge in determined ways, always interacting with other active agents in a system that is nothing but the working out of disturbances.

> "In spring, along gravely stream banks regularly scoured by floods, look for the delicious fiddleheads of the ostrich ferns... Sights disturbed by bulldozers or plows are always worth a close look. For a grand variety of greens, from early spring to summer, visit such disturbed areas frequently... Roadsides offer bounty closely akin to bulldozed areas... In June along a lightly traveled dirt road, you may want to cut poke or asparagus shoots, or pick common day lily buds."[44]

You can't instruct a potential forager on how to find the untrammeled real world, but rather on how and where to find signs that indicate the right kind of disturbance has occurred. Foraging is not about finding the harmonious natural world underneath the cobblestones, it is not about discovering a beach that is just sand, but is instead about the excessive pleasure of upturning cobblestones and throwing them. The beach, then, smells of tanning oil and cream.

You need to make the point that all of the baggage that comes along with the idea of wild plants, whether what attaches itself to these bushes and stems are images of flowers perspiring drips of chlorinated water through the waxed paper of Dixie cups, or maraschino cherries arranged next to a porcelain bowl as on Paul McCartney's first solo album. These images are just as substantial, perhaps more substantial, than the merely contingent fact that the huckleberry thicket on the corner of 47th and Woodstock produces berries that are blue and sweet, but that contain tiny inedible seeds. In fact, these unwanted associations constitute what's real as Philip

---

44) *Elias, Thomas. Dykeman, Peter., "Edible Wild Plants", Sterling Publishing Co., New York, 1982*

K. Dick describes it. The Spectacle is like those inedible seeds or else it's a bone that gets caught in your throat.

Instructions?

1. When foraging for dandelions greens always avoid your neighbor's lawn. They use buckets of weed killer and if some dandelion were to miraculously survive this assault, eating this super mutant dandelion would probably kill you.

2. When foraging for blackberries be aware that city ordinances dictate that these bushes be kept under control, and therefore bushes have a tendency to disappear. What is there in the Spring may not exist to bear fruit in the summer.

3. Those berries aren't outside, cut off from you, waiting in nature. And yet, flowers can never blossom in your head.

4. Wintercress grows in wet meadows, in ditches, or along roadsides. Use early and blanched leaves salads with other late winter foods such as tubers or watercress.

5. Picking fruit should be your first step to picking your battle.

Foraging with Simon

Miriam placed two stacks of blackberry and Oatbran pancakes slathered in real maple syrup in front of Simon and went to fetch him a glass of orange juice from concentrate, while the rest of us served ourselves from the oversized *Blue's Clues* plate next to the stove. She'd made over 20 pancakes and put real butter and a tin of maple syrup down where we could find it. Miriam had even made a pot of coffee just for me (she never drank the stuff), and I balanced my plate of pancakes and my coffee mug and sat down next to Simon at the head of our retro Formica top kitchen table just in time to watch my pale, skinny, and fussy son spit out his breakfast onto the aluminum trim.

"It's not the right kind."

"Did you get enough syrup?"

"It tastes like dirt. Like rocks," he said.

Ben and Emma were quick to scavenge the unchewed pancake from Simon's plate, but even this didn't move Simon. In his opinion the pancakes were inedible, and when I tried to pin down just what it was that he found objectionable, Simon didn't answer but just slipped out of his chair. He leaned back like a limbo dancer, made it past the aluminum trim, and parked himself under the table.

"It tastes like rocks," he yelled up at me.

"I don't understand why you'd say that."

Miriam sat down next to me and then peeked her head under.

"Hi, Simon," she said.

Simon didn't say anything, but Miriam was nonplussed. She took a bite of her pancake and slowly chewed. She made a little face, a tiny frown, and then she spit into her hand. She held the tiny white kernels out to me. "The blackberries are a little seedy," she said.

"What?"

"That's probably what's bothering him."

I leaned my head down under table and watched Simon pick at a piece of chewing gum that was stuck next to where the aluminum leg was bolted into place, and I wondered how long the wad had been there.

"Is that the problem?" I asked.

"What?"

"Are the berries too seedy?"

"I won't eat them."

"It's okay to swallow the seeds. You just have to get used to the texture."

"No!"

The plan that morning was to go wandering and foraging in order to collect more berries. It was late June, but it had been a wet summer so a great many of the blackberry bushes had not yet ripened, but there was enough to merit an expedition. I just wanted to collect enough black berries for a pie, and I'd dehydrate some of the berries as well if Simon would come out from under the table.

He said he wouldn't leave because he was still hungry, but nothing we offered him in place of the pancakes suited him any better. He turned down eggs, toast, and even rejected a bowl of Cheerios. Cold cereal was the only food Simon would reliably eat, but not this time.

"What is the aim of this hunger strike?" I asked him.

"I don't want to go!"

"You don't want to go on a walk?"

"I don't want to forage anymore."

I told him that he didn't have to eat any more berries, didn't have to pick any more fruit or pull up anymore roots, and he didn't have to help me pick words from books or look for the ideas during our walks, but he did have to come along. Everybody was going.

"I don't want to," he said.

"You don't have to want to go," I told him.

Out on the street I tried to remember what it was like to be Simon's age, and found that it was maybe too easy to remember. It was easy to remember what it was like to be six years old because the Woodstock neighborhood with all its houses built in the 1960s reminded me exactly of where I lived in my early childhood. I was not just reminded of where I actually lived, the real suburbia of Denver, but also remembered how the world presented itself to me on television in those days. There was a neighborhood called America and I watched it on television and lived there too. I'd left for awhile when I was in my 20s, lived in a far away place called The City, but now I was back and I was walking the unpaved roads, past basketball hoops and dandelions, and looking into yards for what I hoped might be an escape route.

Walking between green lawns, half rotten wood fences, and overgrown brambles, I found an alley near Steele Street and we scouted for edible plants. We found a huge blackberry bush with ripe berries full of purple juice seeds and we took our plastic bread bags out of our pockets and started picking.

When I was six years old I'd watched hundreds of movies and television programs about the neighborhood of America. I'd seen the teenagers, the sprinkler systems, the robot dogs, and the green lawns. Neighborhood America was easy to get lost in. I used to dream about finding myself walking down streets full of unfamiliar ranch houses and bungalows. I used to be afraid of the lawns and sprinklers that belonged to strangers.

"Robot dogs?" Simon asked.

I told Simon about Valerie Bertenelli. Explained to him that in the 70s, back when I'd been a child, there was a movie about a robot dog who lived in a neighborhood just like ours, and I watched the same scenes over and over again on HBO. I never saw the whole movie, but just remembered that the robot dog could talk and could even swear. Over the intervening decades the half remembered image of this canine full of wires who jumped a chain link fence and sniffed along a curb lined with juniper bushes, this star of a movie entitled C.H.O.M.P.S., took on a certain significance. I told Simon that all the dogs in America were robots—even the real dogs were robots, and all the housewives in all the beige and off-white houses knew the secret. American housewives fed American dogs dead batteries and copper wire when their husbands and children weren't looking.

The words Ben and I had picked for the walk included "husband." The rest of the words on the list were: fantasy, transplant, blood, banana, and sublime.

"Are you sure about the robot dogs?" Simon asked.

"Absolutely," I told him.

Simon picked a seedy blackberry, careful to avoid the thorns, and put it in his mouth. He smiled as purple juice dribbled down his chin and onto his pink Star Wars t-shirt with its sparkly decal of

Luke Skywalker and C3PO.

"There are no robot dogs," he said. He picked another blackberry and stuffed it into his mouth. He was famished.

"No?"

"That's silly."

"How are the blackberries?" I asked him.

He hesitated for a moment, then turned his back to me, and then he defiantly picked another berry and stuffed it in his mouth. "Yum," he said. "Just like little rocks."

Section Four: The Future

The Perfection of Extinction

Miriam's friend Rachel parked her off white Honda Station Wagon in our drive and stepped out of her vehicle with an expression of concern on her face while her two teenagers, Hannah and Wyatt, piled out and let themselves in our front door.

As a single mother of two, Rachel was used to chaos, and she shrugged at the scratch on the roof of her vehicle and then turned to address me. I waved at her from the front door and gestured to her to follow her kids inside.

"Is your wife home?" she asked.

Miriam was gone, either at the grocery store or out picking up chicken feed with our neighbor whose name also happens to be Rachel.

"She's out."

Rachel smiled at me uncomfortably. I told her to stay until Miriam returned, but neither of us had any idea how we'd pass the time together. Rachel smiled at me as she stepped inside but her facial muscles tensed a bit.

Would I be a good host and sit with her in the living room, a terrible option to my way of thinking, or would I ignore her, in which case she'd have to tough it out with my kids while I returned to my office? Neither option seemed quite right.

"You want to help me write my book?" I asked.

"What?"

I wanted to collect more blackberries. It was late in the summer and the bushes of berries that I'd hoped would ripen were withering instead. There wasn't much time left for the huge bush around the corner, for example. "Do you want to see what we can salvage?" I asked.

The bush across from Woodstock elementary had grown through and swallowed up a chain link fence. It stood about six feet high and had produced thousands of berries, but because the bush was so thick most of the berries never received any sunlight and therefore never ripened at all. There were some ripe berries but to reach them I'd had to reach over or through thorny branches and this had meant enduring scratches and cuts on my hands and arms. After a few attempts at foraging this way, I'd opted to see if the berries on the lower branches would eventually ripen. This is how I let the closest blackberry bush to my house go bad.

The seven of us, Rachel with her two kids and me with my three, left the house to forage for the edible blackberry remains. After many scratches and disappointments, we returned with a total of seven good berries in our oversized Tupperware bowl.

"Well that was a failure," Rachel said.

"No. Now I can write from experience about the seasons. Blackberries don't remain available all year. There is a temporal element involved in foraging. Important to remember that kind of thing," I said.

Failure was just as important as success, just as interesting. And I figured I had to keep in mind as much of the context involved in foraging, all the hidden contradictions, as possible if I was going to write something helpful. For instance, I might include the idea that foraging was currently a leisure activity, an activity sustained by capitalist production, and that if people hoped to integrate foraging into everyday life in a new context, they'd first have to produce fruit trees and black berry bushes in whatever was left of the commons.

Rachel smiled a tight-lipped but patient smile. "I'm glad you're working on an ecological book, Doug," she said. But when we reached my house again, after I'd folded the stepladder and returned it to the garage, and after I'd joined up with Rachel and the kids in my kitchen where we all stood watch over the nearly empty green plastic bowl, it struck me that Rachel's tight-lipped smile hadn't softened. Beyond any unease she might have been feeling about killing time with me instead of my wife, something else was bothering her.

"I always knew we humans would kill ourselves off but I didn't think we'd manage to take the whole world with us," Rachel said.

What was bothering Rachel was bothering most thinking people that summer. Ecological disaster was something we'd all grown used to over the decades, but the disaster of the BP oil spill in the Gulf of Mexico had transformed the continual disaster of what I'd liked to believe was our late capitalist era into breaking news. Our general unease had something concrete to latch onto. It was now possible to put an image to this feeling of eschaton. The end of the world appeared as an overflowing toilet deep under the ocean. Shit bubbled up at a constant speed. There was no end to the black bile held deep under the ocean floor.

"Is it worse to think that we might destroy everything as we go?" I asked.

"Of course it's worse. Much worse. I'm thinking of the planet."

"The planet?"

"The planet would be better off without people. We're going to kill everything on it."

"Why would that disturb the planet?" I asked. "The planet could go on without life, couldn't it?"

"Doug!"

I really wanted to know. Once the idea of human extinction could be seen as a positive how much more extreme was it to view the total extermination of life by the same light? "If what you're interested in is a perfectly balanced and harmonious planet then wouldn't a mass extinction be just the ticket? Who needs this infestation called life? A dead planet is clean."

I pressed on. Life itself was a disturbance and in order to restore balance we might as well seek the destruction. Wouldn't this be the ultimate ecological act? If the death of humanity was good, wouldn't mass extinction be better?

"Doug!"

"I don't think you're serious," I told her. "As long as you can think of humanity itself as the problem you're off the hook. It's the perfect way to have your cake and eat it too," I said. "This kind of ecology means feeling guilty about every little thing, and simultaneously enjoying the idea that soon you'll be gone. In fact, in a way you get to enjoy your death now, while you're still alive, as a kind of fantasy of perfection."

Miriam came home at this point, the seven blackberries were gone, but I wasn't anywhere near finished talking. With Miriam's arrival, she had an escape. Rachel's smile softened into real pleasure at seeing her friend at the door, and she laughed.

"Miriam," she said. "Will you help me? You're husband is on a tear again."

"Wait, just because she's home now that doesn't mean you're off the hook."

"Yes it does, Doug." Rachel smiled again. "That's exactly what it means."

Being Gen X: Being Human

By 2010 we Gen X slackers were mostly older than our boomer parents ever imagined they would ever be. We were mid-way through raising our children, and along the way seemed to have forgotten our own history.

Those of us born or raised in the 70s arrived on the scene after the turmoil of the sixties had been transformed into quiescence, and our role models for adult behavior, our childhood memories of how adults behave, are based on this defeat. Bell bottom pants, folk pop, campfire songs, *School House Rock*, and *The Brady Bunch*, these were all memories of co-opted resistance. What was worse was that we were creating our commodified resistance, our own Kodak moments, as we wandered through sunny summer days and felt blades of cool green grass between our toes. We did this unconsciously, telling ourselves that our passivity, our retreat, was our resistance.

We meditated and percolated throughout the zero years. We spoke about dissolving our consciousness, but all the while we were recreating an image of our parents failures. What we wanted to do was collage the past and all its various futures onto our present, not merely out of some postmodern impulse, and not as a symptom of our exhaustion, but in an attempt to disrupt the field of ideology we found ourselves trapped in.

So, we let our kids grow their hair long and run barefoot, we dreamed of untroubled domesticity, of berry bushes and kitchen gardens, of arugula, raspberries, and lemon cucumbers. But this was meant to be only one part of our quiet revolution. Or so we told ourselves.

> "By 1973 Victor Burgin had come to see 'pure' conceptual art as the last gasp of formalism. Art should be concerned with how things and representations relate to one another in the world today (that is to say ideology). Artists must be involved in the world at large. And the central question was 'how could artists intervene effectively in this unceasing flow of ideology?'"[45]

There was a call to return to nature. We were living a life out of balance. We were supersized, oil dependent, television heads who chatted together on Facebook. We were artificially constructed subjectivities who had to learn to surrender to the real. We had to finally put aside our egos and all the left brain chatter that came with them. We had to give up on our plans.

We could see that society was ending, that we were on the verge of breaking the world. But, while we prepared, while we discovered organic, local, healthy, sustainable approaches to consumption, we never took personal responsibility for our individual lives. The tragedy of the totality continued to unfold, but we did not seek any kind of total answer. After all, conscious rational attempts to create a system for living was what had got us into this mess.

In the April 2010 issue of *Adbusters*, Micah White pointed to our dilemma this way:

> "By the time the project of deconstructing distinctions was widespread in academia and had filtered down to society at large, oppression lay not in the maintenance of dualism, but in the opposite—increasing hybridization."

The revolution will not kill your ego. You will not be taken up on

---

45) *Godfrey, Tony, "Conceptual Art", Phaidon, London, 1998.*

the mothership. You won't be slipped easily into the oceanic tumble of a psychedelic vision. Instead you'll be forced more concretely into your own skin as reality slips away and everyday life fades. Say goodbye to the tranquil, adios to surrender.

Don Juan explained our situation, our predicament, directly in *A Yaqui Way of Knowledge*:

> "You think there are two worlds for you—two paths. But there is only one. The protector showed you this with unbelievable clarity. The only world available to you is the world of men, and that world you cannot choose to leave. You are a man! The protector showed you the world of happiness where there is no difference between things because there is no one there to ask about the difference. But that is not the world of men. The protector shook you out of it and showed you how a man thinks and fights. That is the world of man! And to be a man is to be condemned to that world. You have the vanity to believe you live in two worlds, but that is only your vanity. There is but one single world for us. We are men."[46]

---

46) Castaneda, Carlos. *"The Teaching of Don Juan: A Yaqui Way of Knowledge"*, *University of California, Berkeley, 1972.*

Nadine, Brad and the Alexander Technique

The living room carpet was littered with wooden blocks, Japanese eraser pigs, jigsaw puzzle pieces, plastic dinosaurs, and half read library picture books full of elephants and time machines when our neighbor Nadine knocked. I felt ashamed as I opened the front door. I was reluctant to let her in to see the mess. Perhaps sensing this she just stood on the welcome mat and held up an empty wicker basket as a kind of explanation for her visit. She asked if I was interested in foraging for blackberries with her, and while I only had an hour before our family was due to attend a birthday party in another part of Southeast Portland, I agreed. There was just enough time maybe, and I wanted out.

I'd come to know Nadine and her husband Brad that summer shortly after they'd moved into the stucco bungalow next to our ranch house. Simon had introduced me to them. While I spent most of my time that summer locked in my office rewriting my novel, working on this book, or wasting time on Twitter and Facebook, Simon frequently climbed the gray wood fence separating our backyard from our neighbors. He made himself at home on their property, and made friends with them. Brad was an unemployed stagehand and carpenter and he'd patiently tolerated Simon's attempts to help out. Brad oversaw Simon's use of a hammer and the two of them bent green tree branches into armrests for handcrafted lawn furniture. I could often hear Simon's lisping commentaries on their various projects through the plaster walls of my office. Simon would say something very quickly and Brad would repeat what he thought he'd heard Simon say back to him as a question. After 45 minutes or an hour of this back and forth I'd inevitably get up from my desk and attempt to coax Simon back into our yard. Brad needed a break. He was doing my job anyway.

When recruiting neighbors to participate in my foraging efforts, Brad and Nadine had been obvious candidates. They were both actors, they were both a bit younger that Miriam and I while still solidly a part of Generation X. While the neighbors to our south were as bad bets, especially after they installed a privacy fence around their property, Brad and Nadine were open and friendly toward us because or despite of our noisy day to day routine.

"Do you want to forage blackberries with me? I'm hoping to make a pie," Nadine said. She held up her empty wicker basket.

I didn't let her inside, but turned halfway around and shouted. "Simon! We're going for a walk."

"I don't want to."

"Nadine is going too," I said.

"Oh. Hi, Nadine."

She was from rural New York and had grown up foraging juneberries and gooseberries with her two older sisters. Her hippie parents had frequently sent her to school with peanut butter and gooseberry jam sandwiches in a *Muppet Show* lunchbox.

Simon dawdled and dug in the mud looking for toys. He'd found both a green army man and yellow and red plastic cowboy on previous expeditions, and so he poked into the ground with a broken stick as he slowly stepped along. Nadine and I wandered ahead and looked for bushes that still had fruit. I led her to the bushes I'd already surveyed, but we found that most of the berries were brown and shriveled. It wasn't until we'd reached 59th and found blackberry branches hanging over a chain link fence laced with green and white plastic slats that we found ripe berries that were still good to eat.

Nadine and I discussed her work as we picked blackberries. She and Brad had both worked in the Artists Repertory Theater company production of Sondheim's musical *Assassins* in 2009. She'd played the part of Squeaky Fromme and he'd helped build the sets while also playing the part of John Wilkes Booth. After they'd killed the President of the United States, regular work had eluded them both. Nadine said she was hoping to find regular work as an instructor of Alexander Technique.

We picked berries and I stored my portion in my oversized Tupperware bowl. I had no idea what the Alexander Technique was except that it had to do with acting. I asked her about Alexander Technique compared to Brechtian techniques or method acting, but she said that there was no way to make that kind of comparison. The Alexander technique is about the body of the actor and not aesthetics or performance.

In a sense the Alexander Technique is one step beyond the method approach, as it is about the kind of self-awareness and authenticity that can only be achieved through the mastery of the body. According to Professor Tom Vasiliades the Chair of the Alexander Technique department at The New School for Drama (formerly known as the Actor's Studio):

> "Stanislavski [the creator of the method acting approach] understood that excessive and unnecessary tension interferes with creating the spiritual life of the character in performance. The Alexander Technique deals with this directly. Understanding how you do what you are doing in an Alexander way is what Stanislavski spent his life's work exploring."[47]

---

47) *Vasiliades, Tom, "Soul of the American Actor" Volume 7, No.3, Fall 2004*

Nadine told me that bad habits of movement, bad tensions, build up over a lifetime and so the Alexander technique can also take decades, maybe a lifetime, to really master.

"What it was in our society that goes against nature? Why are bad habits easy while natural movement requires such discipline?" I asked.

Nadine wasn't sure.

For Alexander the point of reality came down to the body, the performance, the social realm outside had to be dealt with by returning to one's inner-self through the body. While Classical acting techniques involves mastering proper articulation and learning a vocabulary of emotive signs and expressions and the Method requires that the actor really experience the emotions and ideas he brings out on stage, the Alexander Technique teaches the posture required for the proper articulation of real emotion.

"What about Brecht?" I asked.

Nadine had been in a few productions of Brecht's plays. She'd been in a production of his *Threepenny Opera* and sung Mack the Knife a dozen times, and she'd decided that while Brecht's plays were mostly good, his ideas were terrible. "You're not supposed to identify with what's happening on stage. He wanted to keep the audience disillusioned, alienated, the whole time, but it never worked. Luckily," Nadine said. She was kneeling by the chain link fence, picking berries of a branch that had poked through the slats, and she held up a fistful to me while I bent down with her whicker basket.

I had to stop well before the bush had been picked clean because of the birthday party, but Nadine decided to keep picking.

"Whatever it is, whether it's the reality of the body, the practice of proper articulation, or achieving critical distance it seems like nothing comes easily. We can't just turn to some ready-made nature, or if we do that we'll find that turning takes effort and work," I said.

Nadine reached past the thorn branch to reach some ripe berries that were closer to the fence. She grimaced as she reached back, as the thorn scratched her bare arms.

"See you later," she said.

I nodded, watched her examine her forearm and the thin trickle of blood that was welling up there, and then called after Simon who had drifted down the alley a ways. He was pulling up dandelions.

"Don't pick them all," I said. "I'll probably come back later for some more."

Nadine looked at her arm and then the branches above her head.

"There is no way I could pick them all," she said.

A Food Fight, the Purple Rose of Cairo, and the Wheel of Life

The walls in Annie's kitchen were a muted light green, a green that was almost beige, and everything was well organized. The whole house was like that. She'd managed to transform the kind of thrift store existence that both our families shared into a space permeated with a utilitarian aesthetic. While our house was jammed full of ripped furniture and broken plastic, Annie had placed an Indian blanket on their ugly plaid couch in such a way as to make the sofa work with the room. She managed to maintain the kind of uncluttered and functional home that required work. Just as a return to natural good posture could only be achieved through the constant practice and study of the Alexander Technique, the kind of simple utility on display in Annie's house could only be achieved through constant effort.

She escorted us to her kitchen because that was where she'd laid out what she'd need for the food fight: a large stainless steel bowl of orange Jello, a yellow beach bucket filled with powdered mashed potatoes, and two Tupperware bowls of spaghetti. She'd dyed the spaghetti blue, while the mashed potatoes were colored green with blue number 1 and yellow number 5.

When I wondered aloud about the decadence of wasting food during a worldwide economic crisis, Annie nodded her agreement. The wider ramifications of this party game weren't lost on her, but she'd finally decided that in real terms there weren't enough consequences to warrant denying her son his birthday wish.

"I don't know," Annie said. "It's what Ocean wanted to do on his birthday. It's an inexpensive game, and I'm not wasting any real food. It's all this industrialized garbage."

I couldn't point to any tangible consequences either, but something still seemed not quite right.

"It's not real food?" I asked. "I don't know. I guess I have unresolved ontological issues. I don't know what real food is. The whole idea of the Real is a problem for me."

Annie smiled at this, but some more guests were at the door and our conversation ended there.

Later on when the food fight took place I stayed on the porch, behind the screen door, and did not participate in the screaming, laughing, food colored mess that left clumps of mashed potatoes all over the lawn and Jello stains on the drive, but my refusal was entirely self serving. I preferred not to be pelted with foodstuff, and so I hung back and put a barrier between me and the rampaging children with spaghetti in their hair.

Still, as I watched the fun the question of what constituted real food remained. I decided that whatever problem I was having I'd never understand it by running a cost/benefit analysis. I wouldn't make any headway toward addressing my anxiety if I fixated on utilitarian questions. In practical terms, our individual wastefulness had no impact on, say, the starving people of Haiti. In terms of utility, what mattered was the systemic or structural waste that would continue no matter how well we cleaned our plates or how careful we were with our purchasing habits. The problem with this birthday food fight wasn't real if by real I meant consequential for either the individuals involved in the food fight, or the starving masses.

Splattering the orange Jello on the concrete and grass probably was the right way to maximize everyone's happiness, but who said everyone was supposed to be happy? Guys like Lacan and Freud were suspicious of happiness anyhow, and Lacan argued that fidelity to desire was better than mere utilitarian hedonism. Fidelity to desire could succeed where hedonism failed.

An illustration of Lacanian ethics can be found in the Woody Allen film *The Purple Rose of Cairo*. In the film the protagonist, an ordinary waitress who is trying to free herself from a physically abusive husband and still survive the great depression, falls in love with an RKO movie about an Egyptian vacation, a Madcap Manhattan Weekend, and a heroic archeologist. The waitress is enchanted both with the movie and with the archeologist hero in the movie, and she finds herself returning to the theater in order to escape her miserable life. She watches the movie over and over again and again until, finally, the archeologist onscreen can't help but notice her.

"You must really love this movie," he says. And then in an act of movie magic, Jeff Daniels comes down from the screen to talk to her.

Now, Lacan argued that, unlike happiness, desire is problematic. A person doesn't arrive at his or her desire authentically, but rather is told what to desire by the voice of the prevailing ideological system. Mia Farrow had been taught what to desire by going to the movies, and yet remaining true to these celluloid desires was her only chance at something decent and good. Why? Precisely because her desire was unreal.

In *The Purple Rose of Cairo*, Mia Farrow's fantasy lover became actual but never became real. The impossible perfection of him knocked her off the everyday track of her life, and according to Lacan the ethical act would have been for Farrow to remain true to this disruptive fiction. However, like most of us, when Farrow was presented with a choice: stay with her fictional desire or be happy with a real compromise, she chose to compromise.

In Allen's film Jeff Daniels plays two parts: that of the movie character, and that of the actor who performed the role. When this actor gives Farrow an out from her desire, a way to properly sublimate her desire within the confines of reality, she is opportunistic and seeks this real substitute for her fantasy.

> "Try to understand. You see I'm a real person, no matter how tempted I am, I have to choose the real world."
> —Mia Farrow, *The Purple Rose of Cairo*

Mia Farrow's mistake was accepting the artificial constraints of what passed itself off as "real." Even after witnessing magic, after seeing her desire materialize, she stayed with the utilitarian logic of real happiness.

I stepped back inside the house and, in my usual noisy way, began thumbing through the bookshelves in the living room. What I found was the usual assortment of paperbacks that you might expect (books like *The Epic of Gilgamesh*, *Plato's Republic* and *The Mezzanine* by Nicolson Baker) along with a collection of pop-up books that were unique. I was used to pop-up books for children like Richard Scarry's *Biggest Pop-Up Book*. That book featured worms in trousers, monkeys driving cars shaped like bananas, girl pigs with lunch pails, and foxes who taught alligators and monkeys the letters in the alphabet. In Scarry's book you could make the worm stand up straight by pulling on a tab. You pulled and, bam, Lowly the worm moved from being bent in a chair to an erect position. But, I'd never really encountered pop-up books like the ones in Annie's collection before. These weren't relegated to the children's section, but had a prominent shelf of their own. Beautiful oversized editions illustrating the Louvre Museum, Human Anatomy, Gnomes, and The Twenties through the art of paper engineering, all of them complex and delicate feats of design and sophistication.

But by far the most beautiful pop—up in the collection was the oversized edition of Tibetan Buddhist Mandalas.

This book was not on the bookshelf, but was set open on a shelf of its own, displayed like a work of art. When I came upon it, the book was open to the page of enlightenment. The Buddha was shown sitting on a lotus blossom while an assortment of figures—gods and goddesses of various types—frenetically danced around his serene pose.

Looking up at him I felt the urge to disturb him. I lifted the pop-up book from its shelf and turned away from enlightenment and to the wheel of life.

There was no peaceful center, but only a churning mass of contradictions. Rather than the Happy Buddha there was a red faced monster who held onto a circle cut into six pieces. The wheel of life was the endlessly disappointing quest after an object that didn't exist, and this was good. This was the justification for splattered Jello and mashed potatoes. This image of the messy chaos that was the algorithm of life was the justification and not some calculus of happiness.

I turned the pages of the pop-up book, flipping from enlightenment to the wheel of life, and left the book open like that. And then I returned to the activities in the back yard, arriving just in time for the birthday cake.

Detourning Gondry's "Be Kind Rewind"

For Guy Debord a person's desire is not an unconscious force bubbling up from deep inside, "a force bound to his needs, but is instead conscious and chosen by the individual." The creation of situations, whether through wandering the built environment, detourning newspaper comics, or occupying of factories or universities were thereby attempts to set-up temporary fields of activities that were favorable to these conscious pleasures. Debord railed against structuralists who were, in his opinion, merely attempting to freeze existing social conditions into platonic ideals. However, if one conceives desire as neither sourced to a subject's individual unconscious, nor as independent pleasures that need to be defended or made room for, but as themselves socially produced, then the Spectacle is no longer an illusion to transcend, but another means of production to be seized by the working or productive class.

The surrealism of postmodern filmmaker Michael Gondry's 2008 picture *Be Kind Rewind* offers an alternative to Debord's notion of detournement. Rather than derailing the meaning of a spectacular image through collage or juxtaposition, Jack Black and Mos Def "Swede" them.

"It's a very rare type of video. Sweded," Jack Black explains.

"Like Sweden?" the customer asks.

"Yes."

"That's a country not a verb," the customer says.

"That's why it's so expensive." Mos Def bluffs and wins.

In *A User's Guide to Detournement*, Debord and Wolman describe their revolutionary technique of transforming everyday ephemera such as advertisements, slogans,

Sweding is different from the process of detournement in several respects. In terms of technique detournement takes a mechanical reproduction of a given cultural work and changes its meaning by subverting its content through strange juxtapositions and substitutions. A Sweded movie, however, is altered through an attempt at faithful reproduction of the original by a process of human or handmade reproduction. Detournement attempts to negate the cultural meaning of a work through alteration, Sweding is an attempt to realize the reproduction of culture on a human scale.

Guy Debord offers us a comic strip image with new text in the speech balloon. Imagine Garfield thinking, "From now on we must reassert all the essentially revolutionary demands."

Whereas Gondry, Black, and Def offer us the act of handmade dream production as a kind of liberation. Gondry offers us the seizure of artistic production. According to Gondry's film the process of Sweding must always begin with an act of destruction.

"I'm gonna sabotage the power plant tonight, and you're gonna help me. Look, I got a map completely worked out. We short-circuit this with whatever that thing is, and that blows up … Transform!" Jack Black tells us.

And this act of transformation can only be realized after one becomes aware of how one's own subjectivity is directed and controlled.

"Really? The power plant is controlling us? That's not nonsense?

That's not paranoia?" Mos Def asks.

"Okay, it sounds crazy, and you know why? Because it's affecting my brain too," Jack Black explains. "It's paralyzing it."

In this way Gondry is in complete agreement with Debord. Both Gondry and Debord speak of a conspiracy, and both see this conspiracy as diffuse, nearly universal. They see the conspiracy as the unfolding process of history itself, and as we are interpolated as subjects by and through that unfolding we are implicated in our own domination.

"The TV is malfunctioning. It's not the videotapes," Jack Black explains. "I didn't sabotage the power plant, the power plant sabotaged me!"

Debord said that the highest ambition of the Spectacle is to turn Secrete Agents into revolutionaries and revolutionaries into Secret Agents. Gondry's *Be Kind Rewind* is an aborted movie. It starts down a revolutionary road, but ends up backing away from its own logic. The conclusion of the movie asks us to accept defeat as a kind of sentimental victory. In Gondry's film the power of human scaled dreaming is never opposed openly to the mechanism of control and oppression that dominate the characters. Perhaps the film is meant to be yet another recuperation (an apolitical interpellation of detournement), however, Sweding ends up being so close to detournement that all that is required in order to salvage the technique is to detourn it.

"We'll give them parts to play. This way: A, with their help, we can make more movies and B, the films can be shorter and they won't feel swindled," Melonie Diaz, who plays all the female parts in the movies inside a movie, suggests.

"They're not gonna feel cheated, they won't feel swindled, and they'll see themselves as a part ..." Mos Def repeats her point.

"Yes."

How to Write Instructions on Detournement after Tunisia and Egypt

Just trying to conceive of an approach for a reinvigorated detournement puts you in a doublebind, so the prospect of devising a set of instructions is daunting to the point of being numbing. You're afraid that all you've got to offer a reader is razzle dazzle, and what is worse is that you're pretty sure it's much too late for showmanship. The moment when mystifying explanations could forestall action may have already passed.

Consider this: The demonstrations and riots in Tunisia started over unemployment, food inflation, corruption, free speech issues, and so on, but what sparked the overturning of first Tunisia and then Egypt was the death of a fruit vendor named Mohamed Bouazizi.

According to the official website of the Tunisian National Tourist Office in the UK and Ireland, Tunisia is a perfect destination spot for fruit lovers. Fresh locally grown fruit is readily available at the markets where tourists will find college educated vendors like Mohamed Bouazizi desperate for a pound, euro, or dollar. Pomegranates ripen in October while November is the start of the date season in Tunisia, but Bouazizi was selling apples when he was beaten by a police officer. The apples were confiscated because Bouazizi couldn't produce the proper set of papers, and this rash but small act of brutality is what undid the Tunisian dictatorship.

Bouazizi set himself on fire in front of police headquarters in protest of his treatment and captured the imagination and attention of the Tunisian people. When he died eighteen days later, more than 5000 people participated in the funeral procession.

When his livelihood was taken from him Mr. Bouazizi did not turn to urban foraging, but changed the coordinates of the world through an act of self destruction. It's not an approach you can recommend to readers. It's not even something you, as a trained professional, want to try out for yourself.

Warning. Do not try this at home. Do not pass go. Objects in the screen may be closer than they appear.

Instructions:

1. According to the Situationist International, Greil Marcus, and Wikipedia: detournement is a technique wherein mass produced images are turned back upon themselves. Or to quote the now-legendary group Negativland: "Sounds so big they're never out of view. Boxtop. Boxtop. You can retouch the photograph on the cover of America."

   Despite how impractical it seems, keep thinking about the issue in terms of representation. While you may risk aestheticizing and even trivializing real issues (after all the problems you face don't seem like problems of representation, they seem tangible: Unemployment, environmental collapse, corporate and government corruption, low wages, poor public health, and so on ...) if you hope to detourn anything you'll have hold on to the idea. You'll use words, brushstrokes, chisels, wood, etc ... Go ahead and bend, spindle, and mutilate.

2. Consider the possibility that the philosopher Henri Lefebvre was right when he claimed that space itself is socially produced. It's an utterly quixotic suggestion, and to take it seriously means treating the world like a stage set or television studio. You actually are on *The Truman Show* and

your hometown is *Mister Rogers' Neighborhood*. Still, if you can bring yourself to make believe, Lefebvre's assertion that space is socially produced makes sense. In fact, Mister Rogers and his neighborhood is a good example because Mister Rogers himself was obsessed with workers and production. He took tours of various factories and brought back documentaries that he screened on Picture/Picture. Mister Rogers pointed out that things like crayons, garbage cans, and bass violins didn't just come into being on their own, but rather people made these things. It was the same for nearly everything: crayons, houses, Twinkies, pretzels, puppets.

Once you understand how the objects in our lives are made by people it gets easier to grasp the concept of the production of space. Consider how not only your television set, but also the space a television set occupies, was made by people. For there to be television sets people had to make room for them, just like your mom and dad had to make room for you before you came into the world, and just like their moms and dads had to make room for them, and so on back through the years.

Before there were televisions there was radio, and before radio there was the printing press. In fact, you can track the production of the space for television all the way back to ancient Rome. When Julius Caesar wanted to inform the citizens of his Republic about important social or political events what did he do? He ordered the production of posters which would be displayed on big white boards in cities and villages throughout the Empire. And, in a way, these were the first television screens.

As Kafka once said, "it's enough that the arrow exactly fit the wound."

3. Watch a Will Ferrell movie. No, not *Talladega Nights*, but the film *Stranger than Fiction*. In this movie Will Ferrell comes to

know his life as a representation. The space in which his life is played out becomes unreal to him when he starts to hear the voice of the narrator telling his story. Reality crumbles. While the plot here is similar to *The Truman Show*, *The Matrix*, and *eXistenZ*, the difference between Stranger than Fiction and *The Matrix* is twofold: The first is that the illusion being cast by the narrator is not a purposeful deception, in fact it may not be a deception at all. The second difference is how *Stranger than Fiction* treats space.

This is a story about a man named Harold Crick and his wristwatch. Harold Crick was a man of infinite numbers, endless calculations, and remarkably few words. And his wristwatch said even less. Every weekday, for twelve years, Harold would brush each of his thirty-two teeth seventy-six times. Thirty-eight times back and forth, thirty-eight times up and down.

Harold Crick is perhaps an obsessive compulsive. He is described as a solitary man with no friends, no ambitions, and no fantasies. He is the very definition of the company man, and his one defining characteristic, his need to count and measure the space around, is just another symptom of the emptiness of his life.

In fact, that emptiness is quite literal. Harold Crick is trapped in Kantian or Euclidian space. This is the space of mathematicians and geometrists and, through the revelation of the method, it is the space Ferrell is forced to give up. In this way Crick is made to reenact what, according to Lefebvre, had already occurred on a societal level.

"We've been living without Euclidian/perspectivist space for a hundred years: Around 1910 a certain space was shattered. It was the space of common sense, of knowledge (savoir), of social practice, of political power, a space enshrined in everyday

164

discourse."[48]

Once Harold Crick has come to accept that he is indeed hearing a voice in his head, a voice that is describing what is happening as it happens, he seeks psychiatric help. The psychiatrist, as played by Linda Hunt, suggests that what he is experiencing is schizophrenia. When Crick insists that he really is in a story she recommends that, if his problem is literary rather than psychiatric, he should consult an expert in literature.

Dustin Hoffman plays the part of the literature professor, and while he is skeptical about Harold and his story at first, Hoffman's professor is ultimately convinced when Crick recites a line the voice has spoken. "Little did he know that this simple seemingly innocuous act would result in his imminent death."

'Little did he know.' Did you just say, 'little did he know?'" Dustin Hoffman is elated. He says he's taught seminars about "little did he know." He's dedicated whole courses to "Little Did He Know." But why?

Since Descartes, the problem of epistemology, or the problem of how we know that we know things, has been getting more and more acute. Over the course of the last few hundred years the knowing subject has been split off from the object of his knowledge. "Little did he know" as a theme in literature is an articulation of the split.

The philosopher Immanuel Kant, in an attempt to solve the mind/body or subject/object split, asserted that "space (and time) are not objective, self-subsisting realities, but subjective requirements of our human sensory-cognitive faculties to which all things must conform." That is the structure of space is subjective but real, it is inherent in the mind, and

---

48) Lefebvre, The Production of Space

this structure cuts us off from the real world. On the other hand the idea that space itself might be socially produced is another way to solve the problem. If the story is being told, if the structure of space is not innate but contingent, then while Ferrell is not the source of his own story at present. He has a chance.

4. Turn away from the movie, after all the problem of how to bring off a social revolution isn't a fictional problem or a problem of ideas, it is a problem in your actual life. Or as Harold Crick said in *Stranger than Fiction*: "What you don't seem to realize is that this isn't a philosophy or a theory or a story for me. This is my life."

   The professor answered: "Of course, now just go out and make it the life you always wanted."

5. Answer this question: Who is the narrator? Is it you? It could be, but in societies where industrial methods of production prevail you aren't a single individual, but a class. This class of narrators is currently invisible, unconscious, but is working to become aware of itself. And this process of becoming aware of itself as the productive class that creates space, this is what is called revolution.

Letter to the Talk Show 'Burn'

[The following letter is the conclusion to the Pick Your Battle project. It was written to Michael Franklin, the host of the Blog Talk Radio Program *Burn*, on March 15th, 2011, but perhaps you should read it as if it was written directly to you.]

To Whom it May Concern,

After doping myself up on a bunch of Hollywood movies, skimmed over theories, and some actual dope I've finally figured it all out. Here's our answer: We've got to interiorize the body and exteriorize the soul just like Terence McKenna told us back in the 90s.

> "Our redemption will be the exteriorization of the human soul
> and the interiorization of the human body so that [the body] is
> an image freely commanded in the imagination."[49]

It's a strange, maybe even absurd, idea, I admit, and you have to consider the source. McKenna thought that history will end in 2012, that Psilocybin mushrooms came from outerspace, and that the self-transforming Machine Elves that he saw when he smoked DMT were real. Terence spent a good part of his life stoned on mushrooms, roots, and grass, so it's not surprising that political solutions should appear to him as mystical trips and bizarre visions. Still, I think he's onto something. We don't need to wait for the flying saucer people to land, we don't need any messiahs or spirits

---

49) Terence McKenna, Lectures on Alchemy

to help us, all that has to happen for the human race to end history together and thus have a future is just what Terence said. We have to interiorize the body and exteriorize the soul.

And that's not even the weird thing. The really weird thing is that we've done this already, but we haven't realized it. That is, reality can only exist inside of a fiction, and conversely what we think is fiction is actually real.

Think of the divisions between Nation States on a globe; the way the lines and dots are drawn on maps? Aren't these lines both real and virtual? That is, aren't these lines real because they demarcate real divisions between people in the world? The lines on the globe show precisely how real space and power is divided up, and yet they're entirely virtual, and if you go to look for them you usually won't find them.

One exception would be a place like Four Corners—the spot where Colorado, New Mexico, Arizona and Utah meet. The monument there is exactly the kind of excessive thing that there always has to be when you're dealing with the reality of the virtual. It's a place where fictional borders are made real, a sort of literal *point de capiton*. Lacan defined the *point de capiton* as an anchoring point or a quilting point, and what he meant by this is that a symbolic order, say the symbolic order of states and their interaction, must have points where the relationships are stabilized. But, paradoxically, these points are excessive. There is always a residue of something left over that doesn't really fit into the frame, something beyond itself that points to the limitation or unreality at work. In the exact spot where all four corners meet it's possible to be in all four states at the same time, and it's discombobulating. Everyone who stands on the dot is forced to ask the question: "What State am I in?"

In the case of the monument at Four Corners, the physicality of it is irrelevant. The monument merely represents the quadripoint but it is not the quadripoint itself. Moving the monument would not alter the real location of the quadripoint, and yet, paradoxically, the quadripoint itself is nothing but a representation. If we could move the monument in secret the effect would be the same as moving the quadripoint itself. The monument can only be moved openly through the mechanism of State power, or through some force that could move beyond State power.

I've written to you before about the possibility of Sweding. That is, I want to put together a troupe of actors for guerilla theater projects so that we can create disruptions in the everyday functioning of supermarkets, art galleries, and shopping malls by acting out altered scenes from popular movies in public. The inspiration behind this idea was encountering a YouTube video produced by the acting troupe called Improv Everywhere, and enjoying their reenactment of *Star Wars* in a subway car.

What I want to do is reenact well-known, but altered, scenes from science fiction movies about Time Travel in order to make what's real about these virtual futures shine through. We'll recreate time travelers from *Back to the Future*, *Time Bandits*, *Bill and Ted's Excellent Adventure*, and *Somewhere in Time* in order to make it possible to bring back anarchist/communist messages from our real future.

I even wrote this:

(Marty from Back to the Future is in the produce section of a Supermarket examining apples or asparagus. Doc rolls up with his own shopping cart and interrupts Marty's shopping.)

DOC: Marty!

MARTY: Doc, what are you doing here?

DOC: When I learned that you were in need of sustenance I figured I'd find you here.

MARTY: Yeah, well I haven't seen you since the 90s. What are you doing back?

DOC: I came for you, Marty.

MARTY: Do you need me to go back to the future?

DOC: No, everything is fine in the future. The problem is the present. We have to change the present.

MARTY: I'm not following you, Doc.

DOC: Look around, Marty. Can't you see what's wrong? The supermarket, all of these pears and apples and onions with stickers on them? They've traveled halfway around the world! Obviously the time continuum has been disrupted creating this new temporal sequence resulting in an alternative reality.

MARTY: English, Doc!

DOC: Here, here, here, let me illustrate. (*He finds a blackboard behind the potatoes and stands it up. He picks up some chalk.*) Imagine a future where your everyday life is based on egalitarian principles instead of wage slavery. You follow? This line represents time … (*He draws a line on the blackboard*) … Here's the present, 1985.

MARTY: It's 2011, doc.

DOC: (*He looks at his watch, shakes it by his ear, erases "1985" on the board and then writes 2011.*) This is the future (*he writes "F"*), and this is the past (*he writes "Past"*). Prior to this point in time… (*He points to 2011*) …somewhere in the past, the timeline skewed into this tangent, creating this capitalist 2011. (*Doc draws the tangent on the board and writes "1985-a" on it.*) Alternate to you and me, but reality for everyone else.

MARTY: Everything seems normal to me, Doc.

DOC: (*Slaps his forehead*) Of course, you didn't go with me into the future so this would be your normal present. Right, right. (*He goes to picks up a bag from his shopping cart and takes out an apple.*) Recognize this?

MARTY: That's an apple, Doc.

DOC: Yes, but I didn't get it from the store. I picked it off a tree in the year 2019. In the future there are apple trees everywhere, and strawberry patches. Portland is full of them.

MARTY: So there are still hippies in the future.

DOC: Not Hippies, Marty. Communists.

MARTY: You're scaring me, Doc.

DOC: (*Doc draws a line from the "F" on the board to the point where the tangent skewed into 1985-a. He then takes out a copy of the Communist Manifesto.*) Look! It says, right here, that the weapons with which the bourgeoisie destroyed feudalism are now turned against the bourgeoisie itself ...

MARTY: (*He takes a look at the Communist Manifesto.*) That's the Communist Manifesto, Doc.

DOC: It's a living document in the future, Marty.

MARTY: You mean the past. The Berlin Wall came down in 1989 and the Soviet Union fell in 1991.

DOC: This has nothing to do with the Soviet Union or the past. I told you we have to change the present.

MARTY: How are we going to do that, Doc?

DOC: Trees, Marty. We've got to tell everyone that in the future apples grow on trees.

MARTY: What?

DOC: (*He lifts a bag from his shopping cart, the bag is filled with foraged apples.*) Here, help me pass these out to these ... shoppers.

MARTY: (*Marty watches while Doc approaches another shopper, possibly a plant, and then reads from the manifesto*) "When, in the course of development, class distinctions have disappeared, and all production has been concentrated in the hands of a vast association of the whole nation, the public power will lose its political character." Sounds good to me. (*Marty helps Doc pass out apples*)

These interventions into everyday life, these Sweded scenes, might be something more than propaganda pieces. The aim is to turn supermarkets into spaces that are just as discombobulating as Four Corners. We might make people laugh in the supermarket, but we might also move the coordinates of our collective future a bit. And if we do well we might give the confusing impression that reality isn't Real at all, but virtual.

So, anyhow, will you help me?